The Soul Is a Stranger in This World

The Soul Is a Stranger in This World

Essays on Poets and Poetry

MICAH MATTIX

CASCADE *Books* • Eugene, Oregon

THE SOUL IS A STRANGER IN THIS WORLD
Essays on Poets and Poetry

Copyright © 2020 Micah Mattix. All rights reserved. Except for brief quotations in critical publications or reviews, no part of this book may be reproduced in any manner without prior written permission from the publisher. Write: Permissions, Wipf and Stock Publishers, 199 W. 8th Ave., Suite 3, Eugene, OR 97401.

Cascade Books
An Imprint of Wipf and Stock Publishers
199 W. 8th Ave., Suite 3
Eugene, OR 97401

www.wipfandstock.com

PAPERBACK ISBN: 978-1-5326-6015-3
HARDCOVER ISBN: 978-1-5326-6016-0
EBOOK ISBN: 978-1-5326-6017-7

Cataloguing-in-Publication data:

Names: Mattix, Micah, 1972–, author.

Title: The soul is a stranger in this world : essays on poets and poetry / Micah Mattix.

Description: Eugene, OR: Cascade Books, 2020

Identifiers: ISBN 978-1-5326-6015-3 (paperback) | ISBN 978-1-5326-6016-0 (hardcover) | ISBN 978-1-5326-6017-7 (ebook)

Subjects: LCSH: Poetry—Criticism, interpretation | Poetry—Essays | English poetry—20th century—History and criticism | American poetry—20th century—History and criticism | Criticism, interpretation, etc.

Classification: PS305 M17 2020 (print) | PS305 (ebook)

Manufactured in the U.S.A. JANUARY 2, 2020

To Carine

Table of Contents

Acknowledgments ix
Preface xiii
1. The Poet and Society (with Steven L. Jones) 1
2. Milton's Morality 10
3. Emily Dickinson's Wisdom 16
4. Rilke's God 20
5. Young Eliot and *The Waste Land* 24
6. The Failure of Surrealism 29
7. WWI Poets Reconsidered 36
8. Fancy and Faith in Wallace Stevens 40
9. Robert Frost's Women and Men 45
10. Cummings's Ear 52
11. Gertrud Kolmar's Silent Speech 58
12. What Happened to Basil Bunting? 62
13. Elizabeth Bishop's Artistry 67
14. Yves Bonnefoy's Pursuit of Presence 70
15. André Bouchet's Fragments 74
16. Vernon Scannell's Wounded Music 79
17. Allen Ginsberg, Bore 83
18. Cracks in Language 86
19. The Soul Is a Stranger in this World 89
20. John Updike's Occasional Verse 95
21. Scott Cairns and the Promise of Future Fullness 99
22. Paul Lake and the Politics of Language 103
23. A. E. Stallings's Practiced Movements 108

Table of Contents

24. A Modern Martial 111
25. Flarf and Form 114
26. A Short History of Form 119
27. Is Free Verse Immoral? 123
28. An Avant-Garde Presbyterian 128
29. Orpheus in the Bronx 132
30. Life's Duplicity 137
31. Ernest Hilbert's Street Music 141
32. The Faithful Poetry of Christian Wiman 144
33. Dana Gioia's Articulation 148

Acknowledgments

Many of these essays and reviews were published previously, often under different titles, and revised and expanded for this volume. They first appeared in the following publications:

The Wall Street Journal: "Rilke's God," "Young Eliot and *The Waste Land*," "WWI Poets Reconsidered," "Fancy and Faith in Wallace Stevens," "Gertrud Kolmar's Silent Speech," and "Yves Bonnefoy's Pursuit of Presence"; *The Weekly Standard*: "Milton's Morality," "Vernon Scannell's Wounded Music," "Cracks in Language," and "A Short History of Form"; *The American Conservative*: "What Happened to Basil Bunting?"; *The New Criterion*: "The Failure of Surrealism"; *The Washington Free Beacon*: "Emily Dickinson's Wisdom," "Elizabeth Bishop's Artistry," "Allen Ginsberg, Bore," "A Modern Martial," "Ernest Hilbert's Street Music," "The Faithful Poetry of Christian Wiman," and "Dana Gioia's Articulation"; *Books & Culture*: "André Bouchet's Fragments," "The Soul Is a Stranger in this World," "Scott Cairns and the Promise of Future Fullness," and "Orpheus in the Bronx"; *Chronicles*: "The Poet and Society"; *The City*: "A. E. Stallings's Practiced Movements" and "An Avant-Garde Presbyterian"; *University Bookman*: "Paul Lake and the Politics of Language"; *Public Discourse*: "Flarf and Form" and "Is Free Verse Immoral?"; *First Things*: "John Updike's Occasional Verse." Parts of "Robert Frost's Men and Women" appeared in *The Weekly Standard* and *The American Conservative*. Parts of "Cummings's Ear" appeared in *The Weekly Standard* and *The Washington Free Beacon*.

My thanks to copyright holders for permission to use the material below:

Aaron Belz, "Accumulata," "Avatar" and excerpt from "Ad Infinitum" from *Glitter Bomb*. Copyright © 2014 by Aaron Belz. Reprinted with the

ACKNOWLEDGMENTS

permission of Persea Books, Inc (New York), www.perseabooks.com. All rights reserved.

Yves Bonnefoy, excerpts from "A Bit of Water" and "The Garden," translated by Hoyt Rogers, from *Second Simplicity: New Poetry and Prose, 1991–2011*, copyright © 2012. Used by permission of Yale University Press.

André du Bouchet, excerpts from "Alphabet" and "White Motor," translated by Hoyt Rogers and Paul Auster, from *Openwork: Poetry and prose*, copyright © 2014. Used by permission of Yale University Press.

Scott Cairns, excerpts from *Slow Pilgrim: The Collected Poems* by Scott Cairns. Copyright © 2015 by Scott Cairns. Used by permission of Paraclete Press, www.paracletepress.com.

E. E. Cummings, excerpts from *COMPLETE POEMS: 1904–1962*, edited by George J. Firmage. Copyright 1923, 1925, 1926, 1949, 1950, 1951, 1953, 1954, 1963, 1977, 1991 by the Trustees for the E. E. Cummings Trust. Copyright © 1976, 1985, 1991 by George James Firmage. Used by permission of Liveright Publishing Corporation

Dana Gioia, excerpts from "Words," "The Stars Now Rearrange Themselves Above You," "The Burning Ladder," and "Most Journeys Come to This" from *99 Poems: New and Selected*. Copyright © 1986, 2001, 2016 by Dana Gioia. Reprinted with the permission of The Permissions Company, Inc., on behalf of Graywolf Press, Minneapolis, Minnesota, www.graywolfpress.org.

Ernest Hilbert, excerpts from *Caligulan*, copyright © 2015. Used by permission of Measure Press.

Devin Johnston, excerpts from "Above Ivanhoe," "Ameraucana," and "New Song"; entire poem "Visiting Day" from FAR-FETCHED by Devin Johnston. Copyright © 2015 by Devin Johnston. Reprinted by permission of Farrar, Straus and Giroux.

A. M. Juster, excerpts from *Sleaze and Slander: New and Selected Comic Verse: 1995–2015*, copyright © 2015. Used by permission of Measure Press.

Acknowledgments

Paul Lake, excerpts from *The Republic of Virtue*, copyright © 2013. Used by permission of The University of Evansville Press.

Reginald Shepherd, "God-With-Us" (twenty-seven lines) and "Along with Whatever Has Not Been Named" (twenty-two lines) from *Red Clay Weather* by Reginald Shepherd. © 2011. Reprinted by permission of the University of Pittsburgh Press.

A. E. Stallings, excerpts from *Olives: Poems*. Copyright © 2012 by A. E. Stallings. Published 2012 by TriQuarterly Books/Northwestern University Press. All rights reserved.

Christian Wiman, excerpts from "A Window," "It Is Good to Sit Even a Rotting Body," "Postolka," and "When the Time's Toxins" from HAMMER IS THE PRAYER: SELECTED POEMS by Christian Wiman. Copyright © 2016 by Christian Wiman. Reprinted by permission of Farrar, Straus and Grioux.

Franz Wright, excerpt from "The World" from *The Night World and the Word Night*. Copyright © 1993 by Franz Wright. Reprinted with the permission of The Permissions Company, Inc., on behalf of Carnegie Mellon University Press, www.cmu.edu/universitypress. "Entries of the Cell," and "Crumpled-Up Note Blowing Away" from F: POEMS by Franz Wright, copyright © 2013 by Franz Wright. Used by permission of Alfred A. Knopf, an imprint of the Knopf Doubleday Publishing Group, a division of Penguin Random House LLC. All rights reserved. "Year One" from WALKING TO MARTHA'S VINEYARD by Franz Wright, copyright © 2003 by Franz Wright. Used by permission of Alfred A. Knopf, an imprint of the Knopf Doubleday Publishing Group, a division of Penguin Random House LLC. All rights reserved.

Preface

WHY DO WE WRITE and read poetry? These are two of the guiding questions of this collection, even if they are rarely answered directly. So, let me put my cards on the table here: We do so simply because we are human, and we have been taking the stuff of this world—its trees and dirt, water and rocks—and reshaping them into something else for thousands of years. Don't get me wrong. Art *can* be useful, but utility can never fully explain it. We make it because we can't do otherwise. While poetry *does* tell us, as Rilke put it, to "change" our lives, it doesn't always or even primarily do so. To understand it as a revolutionary tool in the service of emancipation from oppression, for example, is to think of it in the narrowest of terms. Poetry doesn't give *being* to inanimate things, though it is preoccupied with the particularities of objects and people. Nor does it superimpose an arbitrary order on an otherwise chaotic world, even if its patterns cannot be reduced to variations of patterns in the natural world. While not primarily therapeutic, it consoles and reminds us that we are not alone.

Here's another question: who is this collection for? I hope it will interest everyone who loves poetry or who wants to love poetry—from established poets and critics to novices and aspiring aficionados. There are more theoretical essays—like "The Poet and Society" or "Flarf and Form"—that some might find slow going, but the majority of the pieces, most of which originally appeared in newspapers and magazines, were written with a general audience in mind. There is also a healthy helping of pieces on contemporary poets. I hope that these will be useful to readers who are looking for poets that are worth reading but are having difficulty finding any. There is a lot of dead wood when it comes to poetry today—a sad state of affairs brought about by a number of things I won't go into here—but there is also a lot of green life out there. In this book, I focus mostly on the stuff that's living, though I do remove a branch or two.

Preface

The poets covered in this volume are not intended in any way to be a representative survey of modern and contemporary poetry. These are simply pieces on poetry that I happen to have had the time and inclination to write over the past six years and that I thought might serve some benefit to collect in a single volume. Many were expanded. Others were hardly touched.

My tastes are somewhat eclectic, and I hope I'll be forgiven for not taking a side in the battle between "the raw and the cooked" in poetry that never really happened in the first place—at least not for the best poets, who just wrote—but that still preoccupies a few lonely souls. The pieces, except for the first, are organized roughly according to the publication or composition of the work or works under discussion—or the life of the author—because that's how life is: one thing happens after another.

Micah Mattix
Suffolk, Virginia
February 16, 2019

1

The Poet and Society

WHAT IS THE ROLE of the poet in society? In a frequently misunderstood remark, Percy Bysshe Shelley wrote in "A Defence of Poetry" (1821) that poets are the "unacknowledged legislators of the world." Shelley's idea is that poets shape our view of ourselves and the world, which in turn shapes the very course of history since all human action can be ascribed to one or both of these things. Yet, this "legislating" is neither arbitrary nor tyrannical. The poet is dependent on "the true and the beautiful," and rather than impose his merely personal order on others, he tries to "imagine" and "express" the "indestructible order" at work in the world.

The context of Shelley's essay is important. It was written in response to Thomas Love Peacock, who argued in "The Four Ages of Poetry" (1820) that the poet of his day was a "semi-barbarian in a civilized community. . . . His ideas, thoughts, feelings, associations, are all with barbarous manners, obsolete customs, and exploded superstitions. . . . The march of his intellect is like that of a crab, backward." For Peacock, poets like Samuel Taylor Coleridge merely patched together "disjointed relics of tradition and fragments of second-hand observation."

While Shelley's own poetry can be too straightforwardly political, his point in "Defence" is that poetry, at its best, expresses truths that transcend mere "manners" and "customs." Its observations are first-hand and, therefore, never out of date—spontaneity being the guarantor of truthfulness in Shelley's somewhat simplistic conception of artistic creation, which he borrowed, in part, from William Wordsworth. Still, in his view of poetry as an art of truth, not "customs," Shelley is also not so different from Sir Philip

Sidney, who argues in "Defence of Poesie" (1595) that the poet, unlike the historian, is not "captived to the truth of a foolish world" but free to draw a "perfect picture" of unchanging virtues.

What a difference a hundred years makes. Less than a century later, the French poet Guillaume Apollinaire expressed a new, seemingly grander vision of the artist's role in society that would be bad for both poets and poetry. In *The Cubist Painters* (1913), Apollinaire argues, following Nietzsche, that the apparent order of the world is an "artistic illusion." Neither truth nor beauty is immutable. "Truth," he writes, "will always be new." "The monster beauty is not eternal." Form is not *discovered* but superimposed by the artist. This is why Apollinaire writes that without artists "[e]verything would be reduced to chaos. There would be no more seasons, no more civilization, no more thought, no more humanity." In the absence of some "eternal" order, the poet's task is to create a temporary one that transforms our perception of the world and prevents us from getting "bored."

Because of this, new poems and paintings necessarily bring about the destruction of old aesthetic and moral orders. This is radically different from all previous (and most subsequent) conceptions of art as timeless—the idea that great works of art never grow old (and cannot be *replaced* by new ones) because they deal with unchanging human nature. "Picasso," Apollinaire writes, "studies an object like a surgeon dissecting a corpse" (and not, tellingly enough, like one healing a living body). It is no coincidence that at the beginning of the twentieth century military metaphors begin to be applied to groups of artists and art. Instead of "schools" of poetry and painting we have the "avant-garde." In "It's Too Early to Rejoice" (1918), Mayakovsky wrote that "It is time / to pepper museum walls with bullets." In "To Gottfried Benn" (1958), Frank O'Hara writes that poetry is like a nation "at war" when "provoked to defense or aggression."

Of course, truth has not entirely disappeared in Apollinaire's view of art. Art can still tell us about the act of perception and the mechanics of form. Picasso's paintings, for example, show us that perception is, in part, determined by perspective. It is not uncommon to encounter the idea (as I have regularly in reading and in conversation with contemporary poets) that great poems can only be about prosody itself because syntax is the only thing that we can speak about with any objectivity. To write about love is sentimental, but to write about how language shapes this thing we call love and how we give this feeling an inescapably culturally-determined and temporary form in poetry—well, that's supposedly the real stuff.

The Poet and Society

If the form of poetry is not indebted in some way to an unchanging natural (and moral) order but an arbitrary superimposition, it becomes merely a tool of political power. The battle today against "patriarchy" and hierarchy provides a ready-made rationale for the use of parataxis, fragmented syntax, "subversive" punctuation, appropriation (though only certain kinds), clashing imagery, mixing of "high" and "low," and other formal decisions. Such techniques have become so popular today that many young poets mindlessly ape these supposedly subversive techniques (paradoxically enough) in the hopes of getting a tenure-track teaching job—preferably on the East Coast or in California—and settling down to a life of Saturdays at the theatre and Sunday brunches in posh downtown restaurants. This view of poetry and the poet's relationship to society is so widespread that when we speak of a poet's role in society it is almost always in terms of politics—of fighting the oppression of a capitalistic society—even as these same poets hope to benefit from the exchange relationship established by the modern university, as James Matthew Wilson has noted in an excellent collection of essays discussed in chapter 25 of this volume. The poet today—the *real* poet, for most people—should address the masses and call us to arms or chant the Heart Sutra, as the case may be.

In a recent piece for NPR on the Beats, Juan Vidal expresses this view when he writes that for "centuries" poets "were the mouthpieces railing loudly against injustice" and "once served as a vehicle for expressing social and political dissent":

> There was fervor, there was anger. And it was embraced: See, there was a time when the poetry of the day carried with it the power of newspapers and radio programs. It was effective, even as it was overtly political. What has happened?

It's hard to know where to start with Vidal's rather narrow view of poetry. Political poetry did not end with Amiri Baraka, as Vidal would have us believe. Allen Ginsberg may have been popular, but it was more for his persona than his actual poems, and most of the other Beats were entirely unknown to most Americans. (There's a reason Elsa Dorfman's Paterson Society—a proposed reading tour featuring poets like Ed Dorn, Robert Duncan, and Joel Oppenheimer, among others—was scrapped almost as soon as it was started.) Most importantly, however, Vidal's remark that poetry is, and always has been, "overtly political" is patently false, at least in the way that Vidal imagines—"expressing social and political dissent."

THE SOUL IS A STRANGER IN THIS WORLD

For the greater part of almost three thousand years, poets have tended to view themselves not as *maudits* but as men speaking to men, calling others to live according to shared ideals. In Homer's *Odyssey*, for example, the poet does not create his own moral order willy-nilly but embodies ideals based on shared values and observable reality, which, of course, *does not exclude* occasions for correction. In Virgil's *Eclogues*, which was written in the confusing and chaotic days between the murder of Julius Caesar in 44BC and the final triumph of Octavian at the Battle of Actium (31BC), the poet is frank and open about the hopes and heartbreak of the world. At the same time, *The Eclogues* is not presented as either a form of protest or a call-to-arms, but rather a form of consolation. While poetry may "speak truth to power," to borrow a much overused phrase, these works show that it more frequently calls its listeners to remember and to live according to shared ideals, and it consoles.

The Odyssey begins with the poet calling on the Muse to tell the story of Odysseus's difficult return home after the battle of Troy. This convention would seem to suggest that the poet occupied a special place in society as a conduit for divine revelation. The later Roman idea that the poet was not just a *poeta* but a *vates*—a word than means not simply a writer of metrical verses but more accurately a prophet—suggests as much. Yet, in a world in which all events—from the flight of birds to thunderclaps—could be read as divine signs and in which all actions are of possible divine origin, the religious associations of poetry seem less extraordinary. Furthermore, while the poet may have been inspired by the gods, he was not one himself, and always addressed his listeners as fellow men.

At the end of Book 5, Odysseus washes up on the island of the Phaeacians. The daughter of the king brings Odysseus to the halls of her father. The Phaeacians are, for the most part, model hosts. They bathe and feed Odysseus, entertain him with poetry and games, and send him on his voyage home (on their own ships) with many gifts. Except for Broadsea's taunting of Odysseus for refusing to compete in the games (Odysseus eventually silences Broadsea with his great strength and speed), the citizens of Phaeacia treat Odysseus with great respect, even though they do not know who he is at first. The island is an example of civilization. Its citizens are virtuous, excellent in both sports and the arts, courageous, and skilled seafarers.

In Book 8, we have the most detailed portrait of the role of the poet in Greek society in either of Homer's epics. The first thing we see is that while

Demodocus is greatly gifted ("God has given the man the gift of song, / to him beyond all others"), he uses that gift to serve his fellow citizens. After dinner, he is called into the king's hall to entertain Odysseus with a song of "the famous deeds of fighting heroes" during the Trojan War. The poem has the opposite of its intended affect on Odysseus, since it brought to mind the many friends he lost in battle, but the Phaeacian lords "reveled" in it. After the party tries its hand at games, Demodocus is again called on to entertain. This time he sings of love of Ares and Aphrodite. Odysseus "relished every note" of Demodocus's song and the Phaeacians "rejoiced."

Phaeacia is an ideal civilization and Demodocus is an ideal poet, and may even be a figure of Homer himself. His two songs—an epic and a lyric—are representative of all poetry. What we see is that Demodocus has been given this gift to call his fellow citizens to live virtuous lives. In his first song, while Homer does not retell the entire Trojan War, Demodocus praises the bravery of the Achaeans and the wisdom of Zeus, which functions as an indirect call to the Phaeacians to exercise the same courage and humility. In the second, couples who bring shame on the "marriage bed" are rightly ridiculed.

There are many other examples—both positive and negative—of Greek virtues in *The Odyssey*. The lack of hospitality is a sign of the lack of civilization. To be inhospitable is to be a witch or monster. Good wives are faithful, cunning, and patient. Good kings are just and generous. All men should honor the gods, and all men should contribute to the peace and prosperity of the city according to the roles and gifts the gods have given them.

But poetry doesn't only entertain and teach. It also consoles. Odysseus's response to Demodocus's first song, unlike the Phaeacians, as noted above, is to bury his head in his hands and cry. In Book 24, the ghosts of Agamemnon and the son of Melaneus, Amphimedon, whom Odysseus has killed for courting his wife, "trade stories . . . far in the hidden depths below the earth." The point of the exchange is, in part, for Agamemnon, who was killed by his own wife, to praise Odysseus's wife Penelope for her cunning and faithfulness, but the tale also brings some measure of peace to Agamemnon, who suffered so greatly at the hands of his own wife.

The idea that poetry consoles is seen even more clearly in Virgil's *Eclogues*. Set in the bucolic world of Theocritus, it would be natural to expect *The Eclogues* to be a type of escapist poetry in which the poet attempts to construct an alternate world to retreat out of the noise, chaos, and danger of Roman public life. But when one looks closely, Virgil has not avoided engagement with the harsh realities of life but demonstrates instead the consoling role poetry can play amid chaos.

Nowhere is this clearer than in the first poem of the collection, Eclogue 1. The poem is a dialogue between two herdsmen of disparate fortunes. It opens with Meliboeus departing his homeland forever and encountering Tityrus relaxing under a tree making music. The tension in the two fortunes is pronounced. "I leave my father's fields and my sweet ploughlands," Meliboeus remarks, "an exile from my native soil. You sprawl in the shade / and school in the woods to the sound with Amaryllis's charms."

The source of Tityrus's joy is that he has gained his land and freedom back. Land confiscations were frequent occurrences in the dying days of the Roman Republic. Generals looking to disarm their legions were in need of land to give to retiring veterans. The frequent solution was simply to confiscate farms from local landholders and redistribute them. Tityrus had been one of the dispossessed but had succeeded in going to Rome and reacquiring what had previously been his. For which he will be extremely grateful.

Meliboeus responds not with envy but with amazement. All the other farms have suffered tremendously and are greatly disturbed by the political turmoil. Meliboeus goes on to express his personal calamity. While going off into exile from his land, one of his goats went into premature labor, gave birth on hard stone, and abandoned the newborn twin kids. "I'm not jealous of you," he tells Tityrus, "I am merely surprised. All / around the farms are so disturbed. I'm tired and yet I drive my goats on. This one I scarcely drag, / for in the hazel thicket there she's just dropped twins, / the hope of the flock, and abandoned them on the bare flint."

The poem ends in twin speeches of panegyric and lament. Meliboeus and Tityrus both sing Tityrus's fortunate fate that allows him to keep his home and farm. ("Fortunate old man, your fields will still be yours.") The song then turns to the future sufferings of the expulsed. ("But the rest of us must go to thirsty Africa / or Scythia and the rapid Oaxes's chalky stream, / or else to Britain, cut off from us by the width of the world.") They will leave and some retired soldier, a veteran of the civil wars and most likely not a Roman, will inhabit their dispossessed fields. ("Is some rough soldier to have these furrowed fields? / Some foreigner these crops? What misery civil strife / has brought to us Romans! For such as these have we sown / this land.")

The Poet and Society

The final response of Tityrus is telling. He doesn't offer to help Meliboeus solve his problems the way he has his own. He doesn't allow Meliboeus to vent his bile at being so mistreated. He doesn't engage in the trite condescension of the fortunate that "it will all work out for the best" or "everything happens for a reason." There are no political or philosophical maxims offered at all. Instead Tityrus ends the poem with an invitation to sit with him by the fire. ("But still, you could stop here with me this one night, / sleep on a bed of green leaves. I have ripe apples. / Soft chestnuts, and a fine supply of pressed cheese. / And now, over there, the roofs of the farms begin to smoke, / and the shadows fall farther from the tops of the high hills.")

Such a conclusion to the poem reveals Virgil's views regarding the power and place of poetry. Virgil, like his semi-autobiographical self Tityrus (for Virgil had himself regained a family farm lost through political confiscation), offers his poetry not as political propaganda, nor as subversive diatribe, or even as Epicurean retreat from the harshness of reality. Rather, he offers his poetry as consolation. Tityrus doesn't offer to solve Meliboeus's problems. He offers to sit with him, and nourish him, and share his food for the night before he continues on the unfortunate journey that is set before him. The rest of *The Eclogues* might be understood as the fireside songs sung that night by these two herdsman as they contemplate and cope with their diverging futures: songs of death and of tragedy, songs of prophecy and love, songs of humor and hope.

This two-fold function of remembrance and consolation is found in many of the West's greatest epics and lyrics. In Dante's *Divine Comedy*, there's no shortage of uncomfortable truth-telling. Example after example of sinners are paraded before us in *The Inferno* as a warning to the living of the consequences of indulging in sin. Yet, the poet regularly (though not always appropriately) laments the fate of the sinners he sees and expresses his compassion. When the poet encounters the Harpies who have been transformed into thorn bushes, he is unable to speak because "such pity fills my heart."

In *Paradise Lost*, Milton famously (and somewhat provocatively) asks the "Heav'nly Muse" to grant him power in his poem to "assert Eternal Providence / And justify the ways of God to men." There is much assertion and nuanced justification in the poem, but there are also moments of consolation. Book 10 ends with Adam's long lamentation for his sin and for the consequences he now knows it will bring on the world. After this, he turns to Eve and comforts her. "[L]et us contend no more," he tells her, "nor blame / Each other, blamed enough elsewhere, but strive / In offices of love how we may light'n / Each other's burden in our share of woe." While Adam is referring to the consolation of marriage here, poetry too lightens burdens, as Milton knew. In "L'Allegro," he praises the "sweetest Shakespeare" whose "immortal verse" drives out "loathed Melancholy" and "eating cares" and laps the reader "in soft Lydian airs."

In *Lyrical Ballads*, Wordsworth provides a portrait of the English countryside that is both beautiful and full of poverty and death with no solution to such suffering offered other than to "speak" it. In John Keats's "[I Stood Tip-Toe upon a Little Hill]," the beauty of nature "Charms us at once away from all our troubles." Poetry, however, is "[f]ull of sweet desolation—balmy pain" and consoles us with images of "beauty . . . desolate."

The pity that Dante and Milton feel when they encounter sinners is in stark contrast to the contempt and condemnation that many contemporary poets express when encountering modern "sinners." Amiri Baraka writes that white people "cd / be killed / in the right / Situation" and in "Letter to Mrs. Virginia Thomas, Wife of Whatzhisname Lamentable Appointed to the Supreme Court, U.S.A.," June Jordan calls Clarence Thomas "a first class / colored fool / an Uncle Tom" and "brown nose cut-throat." While poets, like all people, can be nasty for no reason, both Baraka and Jordan espoused a "revolutionary" view of poetry (Baraka was for many years a devout Leninist) that gave them *carte blanche* to use poetry as a political weapon against others.

This is not to say that there's no place for satire in poetry—for biting portraits of fools and foolishness. The history of Western poetry is full of such examples. But the modern view that poetry is *only* revolutionary is both new and harmful. It removes the poet from society and sets him against it in a way that undermines community.

In the classical view, the poet is not a Delphic oracle babbling esoteric lines unintelligible to the uninitiated, nor a political mouthpiece of the regime or the revolutionaries, but the companion of the common man, sitting beside him, helping him wrestle with the questions he has, seeking first to understand and give meaningful expression to the problems and experiences and frustrations of life—to hint, suggest, explore, and point towards possible answers. Such poetry, in turn, draws a community together, uniting a society by being the mouthpiece of their hopes and fears. The poet understands and gives voice to the struggles the reader experiences. The reader in hearing his anxieties eloquently expressed feels less alone in the cosmos.

Such a poetry is not entirely absent today, and we can be thankful for the deeply humane work of Dana Gioia, Les Murray, Bill Coyle, William Baer, Christian Wiman, and many others. But we could certainly do with more of the above and fewer of the self-appointed Mayakovskys thundering from the pulpit of the aesthetic, moral, or political revolution.

2

Milton's Morality

IN 2016, DURING THE 400th anniversary of William Shakespeare's death, the Bard was feted by dozens of books, hundreds of magazine and newspaper articles, performances of his plays, lectures, and a Shakespeare Day gala attended by Prince Charles himself. The London Tube map replaced the names of its stops with titles of Shakespeare's plays. Google, of course, did a doodle.

In 2017, it was all Jane Austen—the 200th anniversary of the novelist's death. Like Shakespeare the year before, she was everywhere, not least in the pages of *The New York Times*, which ran some twenty articles on her, musing about everything from what she might tell us about Brexit to why the alt-right loves her so much. *The Atlantic* stated unambiguously that "Jane Austen Is Everything," and it sure did feel that way. Her face now graces the UK's new £10 note.

Pity poor John Milton. 2018 marked the 350th anniversary of the publication of *Paradise Lost*, the greatest epic poem in English and one of the greatest works of Western literature, and hardly a word was said about either the man or the work: just three books have been published—William Poole's *Milton and the Making of Paradise Lost*, John Carey's *The Essential Paradise Lost*, and a collection of essays on the poet in translation—and a BBC Radio 4 documentary.

This rather paltry celebration of a great work and writer is all the more surprising considering the poem has been growing in global popularity. The editors of the recent essay collection, *Milton in Translation*, note that *Paradise Lost* has been translated more frequently in the last thirty years than it was in the preceding three hundred, mostly into non-Western languages. The book "demonstrates that around the world people are taking real interest in Milton," Islam Issa, one of the volume's editors, told *The Guardian*. But in Milton's home country? Not so much.

How did a poem that was lauded even by Milton's enemies as not only above "all moderne attempts in verse, but equall to any of ye Ancient Poets," as Sir John Hobart put it in 1668, and that was translated in its entirety into Latin in 1690 and used in English-speaking classrooms to teach rhetoric instead of classical texts lose so much ground to both Shakespeare and Austen, particularly in Western countries?

One reason is that *Paradise Lost* is, well, a poem, and poems are not only more difficult to read than either prose fiction or plays, they are harder to put on a screen, the reigning medium of our day. There have been dozens of television and film adaptations of both Shakespeare and Austen, but very few of *Paradise Lost*. (A TV version produced by the British actor Martin Freeman is reportedly in the works, but if it ever gets made, don't expect anything close to the original. "*Paradise Lost* is like a biblical Game of Thrones," another of the producers has said.)

The other reason is that *Paradise Lost* is an unabashedly religious work. Early readers, Poole reminds us, shared Milton's belief "in the truth of his subject"—that is, of God, angels, and demons. Like many readers in the seventeenth and eighteenth centuries, John Wesley read the poem devotionally. He even published a religious commentary on it in 1763. Today, however, "the vast majority of readers, both those who defend and those who attack Milton's project," Poole writes, look at the work as merely a "technical masterpiece. . . . This is our view today, and Milton would not like it."

Milton began the poem sometime after 1652—the year he went completely blind and lost his first wife—and perhaps as late as 1658. He finished it in 1665 at the latest. While Milton's nephew, Edward, claimed that Milton dictated the more than 11,500 lines of verse in nearly perfect form in groups of ten to thirty at a time, Jonathan Richardson argued in another early account of the poet's life that he would dictate forty lines while still in bed in the morning and later cut them by half. However *Paradise Lost* was composed, it is a stunning piece of artistry whose scope and complexity have yet to be matched by a single work in English.

Milton's lines can be both digressive and tight, packed with allusions and neologisms. An exceptional student of Latin and a gifted linguist,

Milton coined more English words than Shakespeare, many of them first appearing in *Paradise Lost* (like "terrific," "jubilant," "space" to refer to outer space, as well as "pandemonium"). John Carey writes in his introduction to *The Essential Paradise Lost* that Milton's long sentences, running over several lines of verse, often establish surprising points of comparison. Recounting his first moments of consciousness, for example, Adam notes how both his "heart" and creation "smil'd . . . with joy":

> By quick instinctive motion up I sprung As thitherward endevoring, and upright Stood on my feet; about me round I saw Hill, Dale, and shadie Woods, and sunnie Plaines, And liquid Lapse of murmuring Streams; by these, Creatures that livd, and movd, and walk'd, or flew, Birds on the branches warbling; all things smil'd, With fragrance and with joy my heart oreflow'd.

Carey argues that it is "impossible to say whether all things smiled with fragrance and joy, or whether Adam's heart overflowed with fragrance and joy. . . . What the subtle merging of meaning shows is that Adam is at one with nature. He does not . . . distinguish between what is happening in nature and what is happening in his own heart." Over a thousand lines later, Adam feels a "falt'ring measure" within himself. He goes to find Eve and sees her returning from the Tree of Knowledge with "A bough of fairest fruit that downy smiled" in her hand. The pulling of the branch from the tree evidently ruptured Adam's heart even before he tastes its fruit.

Key words are also repeated but change in meaning as the narrative progresses. Carey remarks, for example, that when "lapse" is first used it refers to the innocent movement of streams. After the fall, however, it "comes to signify original sin, and the loss of man's freedom that goes with it":

> "Maze," "error," "serpent" and "wandering" are other words that fall. When, at the creation, God separates land and water, the rivers, "with serpent error wandering" are innocent, so are the brooks in Paradise that run "With mazy error under pendant shades." But once sin has entered the world these words are overtaken by evil. The devils in hell debate philosophy, "in wandering mazes lost."

We see this use of doubling in the structure of the poem, as well. The first ten books of the poem, as David Quint has observed, mirror each other in meaningful ways. Beginning *in medias res*, shortly after God has cast Satan out of heaven, the poem follows the Devil's "rise" as chief enemy of God in the first three books, culminating in his provocative offers to "save" his fellow demons, as well as his daughter, Sin, and his son, Death, by bringing destruction to God's creation. This "rise" is mirrored in Adam and Eve's fall in books 8 to 10. Book 4 offers Eve's account of creation; book 7 offers Adam's. The middle books—5 and 6—recount the war in heaven. Thus, we have a sort of circle, moving from Satan's expulsion from heaven in book 1 to Adam and Eve's removal from Eden in book 11, with the war in heaven at the core. It seems fitting, too, that the final two books of the poem—11 and 12—address the future judgment and redemption.

The point of all this mirroring is to show how closely evil resembles good. Poole writes in *Milton and the Making of Paradise Lost* that Milton "regards evil as disarmingly close in appearance to the good," and it is only by careful moral reasoning that the two can be separated. Shortly after Milton returned from Italy in 1639, where he met Galileo and spent several months participating in various Florentine literary salons, he wrote in his commonplace book, "In moral evil much good may be mixed, and that with singular craft."

Notwithstanding Milton's famous promise in the opening section of the poem to "assert eternal providence / And justify the ways of God to men," it is Satan's poem from beginning to end. He is the first character to speak, and he is eloquent, bold, full of feeling for others. His first words are ones of consolation for his fellow fallen angel Beelzebub: "O how fall'n! how changed / From him who in the happy realms of light / Clothed with transcendent brightness didst outshine / Myriads, though bright!" He follows this with a word of encouragement: "All is not lost: th'unconquerable will / And study of revenge, immortal hate / And courage never to submit or yield— / And what is else not to be overcome?" He promises the other demons that he will never yield to God's tyranny and tells Sin, with whom he had relations after she burst from his head Athena-like, that he will set her and her son free from "this dark and dismal house of pain" and, like a loving husband and father (at least until the mask slips), provide a home where "ye shall be fed and filled / Immeasurably: all things shall be your prey!"

The poet Percy Bysshe Shelley praised Milton's Satan as "a moral being . . . far superior to his God . . . who perseveres in some purpose which he has conceived to be excellent in spite of adversity and torture." The problem is that Satan's "excellent" purpose is the destruction of "harmless innocence" for personal and political ends. This makes him, Carey writes, "English literature's first terrorist."

In short, Satan says all the rightly compassionate things but only to the "right" people, who are, of course, his people, and only when his own interests are at stake. He is unflappable only in front of a crowd, courageous only when it is personally advantageous. He acts like a good leader, father, and husband—and even argues with nearly perfect reasoning that he is more morally upright than God himself—all while serving only himself. He is a god of unchecked liberty, and, therefore, in Milton's view, a god of chaos and destruction.

What is particularly chilling about the character of Satan is the extent to which he believes all his actions, no matter how violent, are not only justified but morally right. C. S. Lewis write that "we see in Satan . . . the horrible co-existence of a subtle and incessant intellectual activity with an incapacity to understand anything," particularly his own selfish motivations. Satan wants the freedom to do as he pleases, but it is a freedom that always comes at the expense of others' liberty.

Milton, of course, was something of an individualist himself. He wrote in defense of the freedom of the press and divorce and was one of the few supporters of the abolition of the monarchy in favor of executing Charles I. He served as secretary for foreign tongues to the council of state in Cromwell's Protectorate. It's strange, then, that Satan often sounds like a republican. In book 1, he speaks out against monarchical tyranny and he democratically offers his fellow demons a chance to travel to Eden to destroy God's creation.

But like everything else that Satan does, the offer is a façade. Unsurprisingly, no one volunteers after Satan's bleak description of the "perilous attempt," and he quickly chooses to do it himself, thus showing himself of "highest worth" and solidifying his authority over his peers. In book 12, after the archangel Michael tells Adam about the Tower of Babel, Adam laments that his progeny, following Satan's example, will desire to raise themselves above their peers and assume "[a]uthority usurped from God not giv'n." Michael responds that political tyranny is the direct result of men neglecting to rule their own liberty with reason and using that liberty instead to pursue "upstart passions":

> Reason in man obscured or not obeyed
> Immediately inordinate desires
> And upstart passions catch the government
> From reason and to servitude reduce
> Man till then free.

Today we prefer a simpler moral reasoning. We are taught to trust our feelings and to believe that bad people are obviously bad and good people are obviously good. Avoiding evil is merely the result of staying informed, not discernment, of "raising awareness" on social media or with a Friday-night protest. *Paradise Lost* shows otherwise.

3

Emily Dickinson's Wisdom

A POPULAR APPROACH TO Emily Dickinson's poetry is to read it as a subtle critique of patriarchy. Her frequent dashes supposedly mark a fissure in the poet herself. She is a woman who—at least internally—does not live according to nineteenth-century definitions of womanhood. Her rejection of tradition is found in her occasionally irregular meter and off rhymes. Her elegies undermine the "male pastoral elegy," as one critic put it, and her religious verse questions God's "jealousy" and the reality of judgment.

There's a kernel of truth in this. Dickinson could certainly be slyly subversive of both social conventions and religious belief. But to read her only as some sort of proto-feminist is rather narrow, to say the least. It binds her to men, ironically enough, more tightly in death than she ever was in life and can create the impression that her poetry is valuable only to the extent that it expresses a contemporary view of womanhood. Worse, it smooths out the eccentricities of one of America's most idiosyncratic poets with the jack plane of "theory."

Reading Dickinson closely, however, is to find delight in odd metaphors and strange sounds in poems that oscillate between whimsical riddle and hard-nosed philosophical meditation. Dying daisies ooze in "crimson bubbles / Day's departing tide," she writes in one poem. In another, she takes note of "The Cordiality of Death." She imagines her brain flying out of the top of her skull in another and remarks that "The fellow will go where he belonged— / Without a hint from me, // And the world—if the world be looking on—/ Will see how far from home / It is possible for sense to live."

In still another, education is compared to the "Dark Sod" through which a "Lily passes sure."

Dickinson was a pastoral poet. Her poems are filled with flowers, robins, and butterflies, and, of course, the sun. It rises, in one poem, "A Ribbon at a time!" In another, it burns to death: "Blazing in Gold—and / Quenching—in Purple! / Leaping like Leopards to the sky— / Then—at the feet of the old Horizon— / Laying its spotted face—to die!" But she was also a stoic, facing the sometimes terrifying world with composure and wisdom expressed in maxims and tightly constructed arguments. Her poems can read like a collection of (sometimes heterodox) psalms and proverbs. She is, at times, to risk a bit of patriarchy, an American Marcus Aurelius.

A recurring idea in her poetry is that our experience and understanding of a thing is heightened as much by its absence as by its opposite. "Water, is taught by thirst," she writes in one poem:

> Land—by the Oceans passed.
> Transport—by throe—
> Peace, by its battles told—
> Love, by memorial mold—
> Birds, by snow.

And poetry by silence, one wants to add. This is not an uncommon idea. Ancient rhetoricians knew this. So did Keats, who argued in "Ode to Melancholy" that joy and melancholy are co-dependent emotionally and linguistically and, therefore, co-sovereigns of our psyche ("Aye in the very temple of Delight," he writes, "Veil'd Melancholy has her sovran shrine"), equal in power and value. And post-structuralists stake their academic careers on this idea. For Dickinson, however, while the word and idea of water are inexorably linked to the word and idea of thirst, this does not mean that the two are morally equivalent. There is a hierarchy of value. Thirst helps us to know water, not the other way around, because water is greater than thirst. Anguish teaches "Transport," not the other way around, because joy is greater than suffering. The horror of war helps us to grasp the value of peace; memory, love.

This is all fine and good until we get to that last, beguiling line: "Birds, by snow." There has been a shift—at least it seems—as Dickinson moves from the emotional world of joy, peace, and love to the physical one of birds. How does snow "teach" birds? Snow makes apparent, perhaps, the color of birds, which stands out against the snow's whiteness. The quietness of snow may highlight the small sounds birds make; its deathly stillness, the birds' lively movements. In this last reading, however, one could take "birds" as a symbol of life and "snow" as a symbol of death, which would square with Dickinson's use of "teach" to make a distinction between superior and inferior things. Life is better than death, as home ("Land") is better than its absence ("Oceans passed").

For Dickinson, comparing things also helps us to know the multifaceted particularities of each. Making a moral distinction between life and death or peace and war does not obliterate the distinctiveness of either life or death, peace or war, but increases it. Take "[There's a certain Slant of light]," for example:

> There's a certain Slant of light,
> Winter Afternoons—
> That oppresses, like the Heft
> Of Cathedral Tunes—
>
> Heavenly Hurt, it gives us—
> We can find no scar,
> But internal difference—
> Where the Meanings, are—
>
> None may teach it—Any—
> 'Tis the Seal Despair—
> An imperial affliction
> Sent us of the Air—
>
> When it comes, the Landscape listens—
> Shadows—hold their breath—
> When it goes, 'tis like the Distance
> On the look of Death—

As we saw above, Dickinson shows us that our understanding of what things are depends on attentive comparison. It is only in comparing various "slants" of light at various times of year that the speaker in the poem comes to understand the difference between the rays and the "internal" differences that these phenomena create. It is the task of the poet to make these comparisons, note the differences, and name things rightly. Dickinson does this repeatedly in her work. "The difference between Despair / And Fear—is like the One / Between the instant of a Wreck— / And when the Wreck has been," she writes in one poem. In another: "Pain—has an Element of Blank— / It cannot recollect / When it begun—Or if there were / A time when it was not." In still another: "Suspense—is Hostlier than Death— / Death—tho'soever Broad, / Is just Death, and cannot increase— / Suspense—does not conclude."

But she also reminds us that things can mean more than one thing. Light can be both a source of life and death and, therefore, can be a figure of both God's life-giving truth and violent judgment. It can be—depending on the slant—a welcome ray of warmth or a stinging brightness that forces us to keep our heads down. She's in good company in understanding light in this way. The psalmists say much the same thing. We read this in Psalm 43, for example: "Send out your light and your truth; / let them lead me; / let them bring me to your holy hill / and to your dwelling!" But in Psalm 94, we have this: "O Lord, God of vengeance, / O God of vengeance, shine forth! / Rise up, O judge of the earth; / repay to the proud what they deserve!"

While Dickinson revels in the beauty of nature (she is, as she put in one of her most anthologized poems, and one of the few to be printed in her lifetime, a "Debauchee of Dew"), she also writes against a too-strong attachment to this world and recommends the suppression of desire. "Undue Significance a starving man attaches / To Food—," she writes in one poem, "Partaken—it relieves—indeed— / But proves us / That Spices fly." Like the Stoics, she regularly claimed not to fear death (as above) and praise those that died honorably. "It may be—a Renown to live—," she writes in a poem on the Civil War, "I think the Men who die— / Those unsustained—Saviors— / Present Divinity—."

Her relationship to God was complex. Unlike her father and sister, she never made a profession of faith that we know. In some poems she longs for God's mercy. "Papa above!," she writes in an early poem, "Regard a mouse / O'erpowered by the Cat! / Reserve within thy kingdom / A 'Mansion' for the Rat!" In others, she lashes out at what she views as God's overly high demands and pettiness.

And she could be coy. "To fill a Gap," she recommends playfully in one poem, "Insert the Thing that caused it." But mostly she is strikingly original and wise over nearly 1,800 poems—an astonishing accomplishment that is even more astonishing when we remember that she wrote most of them in near isolation.

4

Rilke's God

IT IS FAIR TO say that the German poet Rainer Maria Rilke was bedeviled by God or by what he called God. In "Improvisations of the Caprisian Winter" (1906–7), for example, God is a mountain, Rilke writes, in which "I climb / and descend all alone and lose the way." In another early, uncollected poem (1909), he addresses God as "you, whom I cannot take hold of now, anywhere."

For Rilke, God is difficult to grasp not because he is absent per se but because he has been pushed to the corners of our mind. "Could one not see the history of God," Rilke writes in one of his two "Letters on God," recently published in English for the first time, "as if it were the side of the human condition that was never visited, always put off, saved up for later, and eventually missed out on altogether?" The poet's duty is to find him again.

Annemarie S. Kidder's translations of these two essay-like letters on God show how central this search was to the poet. The first was written in Munich on Nov. 8, 1915, not long after the French blockade of the city during World War I. Writing to a female admirer of his only novel, *The Notebooks of Malte Laurids Brigge* (1910), Rilke, perhaps with the war at the forefront of his mind, quickly turns to the question of how it is possible to live when life is so "incomprehensible."

It isn't, he answers, unless we embrace all that is beyond our control, including death. We wrongly treat death as unnatural, Rilke argues. We bracket it out when we should accept it as part of the cycle of life. "When a tree begins to bud," Rilke writes, "both death and life spring up in it." To embrace death is to embrace the "incomprehensible," which, for the poet, is another name for God.

Rilke was raised a Catholic, and there are echoes in his work of Christ's pronouncement that "whoever loses his life for my sake will find it." Yet, he came to reject the Catholic church due to what he saw as his mother's superficial religiosity. Sophia Rilke (née Entz), who came from a well-to-do family in Prague, would often take the young Rilke on pilgrimages and to churches. If the family could not be wealthy, they could at least be "spiritual," she seems to have believed. While the poet was deeply attached to his mother in his youth, he came to despise her overbearing nature and what he called "her absent-minded piety." In his poetic cycle *Visions of Christ* (1896–98), which he refused to publish in his lifetime, Rilke rejects the principle tenet of the church—the divinity of Christ—fashioning instead his own sense of spirituality.

In his second letter on God, written in 1922 in the guise of a factory worker and addressed to the deceased poet Emile Verhaeren, Rilke asks: "Who is this Christ that is meddling in everything?" For Rilke, Christ is holy to the extent that he embraced death and, therefore, life. He is a mere example of a life fully lived. "I cannot believe," the poet writes, "that the cross was meant to remain; rather, it was to mark the crossroads." People who worship Christ, Rilke writes, are "like dogs that do not comprehend the meaning of an index finger and think they have to snap at the hand."

For Rilke, "degraded Christianity" has wrongly disdained sex, which has resulted in its "distortion and repression." His own version of Christianity celebrates boundless sex as a form of participating in the mystery of one's own life. (This is a view, no doubt, that was at least a little convenient for a poet who, to put it delicately, maintained a number of complicated relationships with women.) He comically lauds in this letter the debauched popes "weighed down by illegitimate children, mistresses, and victims of murder." "Was there not more Christianity in them," Rilke asks seriously, "than in the lightweight restorers of the Gospels; namely, something alive, unstoppable, transformed?"

As these letters show, Rilke's search for God was really a search for self. In finding himself, the poet hopes to find what he calls God but what most Christians would call devilry. His rather strange definition of death as part of God helps to make sense of Rilke's most powerful poetic sequence, *The Duino Elegies* (1923). In his earlier poems, God had been our "neighbor" who hides in "lowly" places. The poet watches attentively for the divine being's "groping hand." But in *The Duino Elegies*, God is replaced by a powerful angel, who represents death and who the poet must *confront* in order to *create*.

"Every Angel," Rilke writes in the first elegy, "brings terror." Therefore, he, at first, looks elsewhere. He looks to women and music in the first elegy. He hears voices. "What do they want of me," he asks, and considers "speaking" of those no longer "with us," but remarks that the dead have no need of the songs of the living. In the second elegy, he reflects on the finality of death, and in the third, on the temporary power of love. In the fourth and fifth, he turns to symbols—dolls and puppets—but realizes that symbols too die. He asks the angel if there is a "place" where "lovers" who failed in life might "show" a perfected scene to an audience of "silent dead." In the sixth, he considers the image of a fig tree and that of a "hero" who rises in "Being," but who is "sung" by fate in "the tempest of his blustering world." In the seventh, the poet sings about the life and power of nature, and in the eighth he compares the beautiful ignorance of animals vis-à-vis death with man's ever-present consciousness of it.

This brings us to the final two elegies. Why is man, Rilke asks at the beginning of the ninth elegy, aware of *both* the beauty of life and the emptiness of death? Is it, perhaps, because without this awareness of death man would not be able to "name" life and, therefore, give a temporary fullness of being? "Are we *here*," Rilke writes in a famous passage, "just to say: / house, bridge, well, gate, jug, fruit tree, window." This is not the poet speaking as a man created *in the image* of God but the poet speaking *as* God—the divine being who speaks things into a sort of existence. The "things" of the world, Rilke writes, "wish us to / transmute them / in our invisible heart—oh, infinitely into us! / Whoever we are." It is death that makes us aware of the "surplus of existence." This is its "sacred revelation." In the final elegy, the poet visits the City of Pain, which is made of the world's suffering, and seems to be set on a hill. He speaks with the angel who tells him about the city. The two—angel and poet—embrace, and the poet turns to climb the mountain of suffering alone (the artist always must suffer alone in Rilke), transforming his pain, it is implied, into art.

This is, ultimately, a tragic view of art, and one that remains popular today, where the artist must choose life over death in his work even though there is no reason for doing so. He speaks as a divine being—the only divine being in the world—and gives the world a temporary "presence" through his art. He is a sort of Christ figure, "redeeming" the world through suffering, but, again, that redemption is always only temporary. Death has the final word, and so it does in *Duino Elegies*. Poets show us, he writes, we who think only of "rising happiness," to know what it feels like when "a happy Thing *falls*."

5

Young Eliot and *The Waste Land*

The poet E. E. Cummings once remembered the young T. S. Eliot as "a snob, cold," and "aloof." He wasn't alone. When Bertrand Russell introduced Eliot to Lady Ottoline Morrell in 1916, she was disappointed to find him "very formal." Virginia Woolf wrote in her journal after meeting him in 1918 that he was a "polished, cultivated, elaborate young American," though she sensed that this exterior hid a man with "strong views" and a "poetic creed." Eliot was a "shy, sometimes naïve and vulnerable" young man, Robert Crawford notes in *Young Eliot* (2015), a biography of the poet's early years, whose poetry—particularly *The Waste Land*—was shaped by personal suffering.

His childhood was happy and unremarkable. He grew up in a stern and loving home where propriety mattered as much as morality. ("When I was a small boy," he once recalled, "I was reproved by my family for using the vulgar phrase 'O.K.'") That family was of respectable Massachusetts Unitarian stock. They could trace their origins back to John Winthrop's Massachusetts Bay Colony, and Eliot's paternal grandfather, who moved to St. Louis in 1834 to start the first Unitarian church west of the Mississippi and later founded Washington University, was dubbed the "Saint of the West" by Ralph Waldo Emerson.

The youngest (by far) of six children, Eliot had few friends, owing partly to his shyness and partly to the lack of what his parents viewed as suitable playmates in the family's deteriorating downtown neighborhood, where they remained to tend to Eliot's grandmother until she died in 1908. Eliot was also born with a congenital double hernia and wore a truss,

Crawford tells us, which prevented him from playing sports and roughhousing with other boys.

He was close to his mother, who published conventional poetry in the Unitarian church magazine, and his Catholic nurse, Annie. As he grew, he came to love dancing (as a young adult, he would "roll back the carpets of his London flat and foxtrot with his wife") and developed a lifelong fascination with the sea. In Gloucester, Massachusetts, where the family vacationed every summer, Eliot learned to swim and sail. In summers during his college years, he would often navigate past the Dry Salvages, a group of three rocks with a beacon off of Cape Ann, and once almost went as far as the Canadian border in a "19-foot knockabout," according to one of his classmates. The third of Eliot's *Four Quartets* is titled "The Dry Salvages," and references to water and the sea are sprinkled throughout his work.

At Harvard, Eliot was still shy and held on to his Unitarian propriety in some areas while casting it off in others. He joined the Digamma (or Fox) Club, an exclusive social and dining club for Harvard undergraduates founded in 1898, in his sophomore year and eventually became the club's treasurer, librarian, and official balladist. Eliot made himself popular with his fraternity brothers when, charged with writing a poem to accompany the club's notoriously boozy dinners, Eliot wrote the "Columbo" and "King Bolo" poems, which were sexually explicit and racist.

It's hard to know what to make of these aspects of Eliot's work. Crawford, for example, suggests that the writing of scurrilous poems was a way for Eliot to compensate for his social awkwardness and rebel against his parents' "genteel" Unitarianism, yet he remained inexperienced with women.

After graduation, Eliot spent a year in Paris before returning to Harvard to begin doctoral work in philosophy. He met Emily Hale in 1912 and fell in love. After two years, Eliot finally told her his feelings, but she rebuffed him. Eliot was crushed. He continued to think about her for many years, and the two would begin a thirty-year correspondence in 1927.

Eliot's trip to Oxford for a one-year fellowship in late 1914 would mark the beginning of his permanent residence in England. Shortly after he arrived in August, he saw Bertrand Russell, whom he knew from Russell's visit to Harvard earlier that year. He met Ezra Pound in September and Vivien Haigh-Wood in March 1915. Three months later and without their parents' knowledge, Eliot and Haigh-Wood were married.

According to Crawford, Eliot's life with Haigh-Wood and their troubled relations are inextricably linked to *The Waste Land*. Things were difficult from the beginning. Haigh-Wood became ill shortly after the wedding, and Eliot had to find a job. She then had an affair with Russell as early as the couple's first year of marriage. Russell, who liked Eliot and often helped the couple financially, had his eyes on Vivien from the moment Eliot introduced him to her. Russell's self-serving justifications to friends who knew of the affair are wince-inducing. In a 1916 letter to his lover, Lady Constance Malleson, Russell explained his interest in Vivien in purely noble terms: "The root of the matter is that she had become filled with fear through having been hurt, and out of defiance had become harsh to everyone including her husband, who is my friend, whom I love, and who is dependent on her for his happiness. . . . I am really vitally needed there, and one can't ignore that."

While Haigh-Wood was demanding, unstable, and manipulative, she was also one of her husband's greatest supporters, regularly telling others how great his poetry was and helping him with editing and correspondence. For his part, Eliot responded to Haigh-Wood's increasing neediness by working longer hours and cutting himself off from her. In 1925, he wrote that "In the last ten years—gradually, but deliberately—I have made myself into a machine. I have done it deliberately—in order to endure, in order not to feel—*but it has killed V.*"

Without denying its "resonances" and "social criticism," Crawford writes that *The Waste Land* is also "a lasting cry, giving voice to a darkness deep in the human psyche." The use of images associated with fertility rites, the dead spring of the opening section, and the poem's moments of miscommunication, paranoia, and frustration reflect to some degree Eliot and Haigh-Wood's relationship. Pound linked the poem to Eliot's sex life, suggesting that it represented an "exuding" of "deformative secretions," and Eliot himself remarked a decade after its publication that "To me it was only the relief of a personal and wholly insignificant grouse against life."

This may be true, but the poem's meaning, as Crawford knows, cannot be reduced to its root in the poet's personal life. "Were *The Waste Land* only the poetic lament," Russell Kirk writes in *Eliot and His Age* (1971), "of a man whose marriage had not fulfilled his hopes, and who had worked himself to the bone, it would remain interesting—but it could not have spoken as a conscience to a multitude of other consciences. A widespread decay of love is no accident." Eliot, Kirk suggests, addresses not only his own loveless marriage and sense of alienation from his wife in the poem, but the widespread loss of love and increasing alienation in a world that has been transformed by materialism. The old orders of church and family had been broken by a long attack from a narrow secular rationalism and individualism. However, it quickly became apparent to some that sex without the obligation of love, work freed from all filial responsibilities, art broken from tradition, and ethics without God created only a temporary sense of exhilaration. The First World War showed that the utopian dreams based on some sort of pure rationalism and enabled by technology could become a nightmare.

Kirk understands the poem as enacting a kind of recovery of the old orders in Eliot's allusions to a version of the Grail legend, where a knight or knights enter Chapel Perilous, ringed by tombs, to discover a cup, lance, sword, and stone. "If they found the hardiness to inquire, they would be answered. . . . And of that questioning great good would come: the Fisher King's wound would be healed, and the desolate land would be watered again." "So in a civilization reduced to 'a heap of broken images,'" Kenner remarks in his study on Eliot, *The Invisible Poet* (1959), which Kirk cites, "all that is requisite is sufficient curiosity; the man who asks what one or another of these fragments means . . . may be the agent of regeneration."

The poem opens, Kirk argues, with the speaker remembering the old aristocratic order (figured in the person of Marie), comparing it to the new (figured in the dead of the "Unreal City" walking over London Bridge), and wondering, albeit indirectly, if there is any escape—if new life, a coming spring, is possible. April is the "cruellest month" because the hope of new life that spring evokes is, at least for Eliot at the time, like Rilke, always temporal. Unfulfilled hope is the worst sort of pain, which is why the speaker of the poem initially claims that it is preferable to live in winter, covered in "forgetful snow."

Yet the rest of the poem is largely an act of remembering, as lines, characters, and scenes from the Bible, *The Divine Comedy, Metamorphoses, Les Fleurs du mal*, Augustine, Spenser, and Shakespeare are contrasted with overheard conversations in pubs and parlors. The contrast between the richness of Eliot's allusions to great works of the past and the flatness of contemporary discourse on sex and money shows the impoverishment of contemporary understanding of human relationships in which everything is an exchange ("Now Albert's coming back, make yourself a bit smart. / He'll want to know what you done with that money he gave you / To get

The Soul Is a Stranger in This World

yourself some teeth"). But the great lines recalled don't enter the everyday lives of the characters in the poem. They inhabit two different worlds and speak in two different languages—the former committed to elegance and governed by duty, the latter imprisoned by eroticism and expediency. This may be oversimplifying the contrast somewhat—Eliot knew as well as anyone that great writers and works of the past on occasion turned to eroticism and recommended expediency. Still, Eliot's impression, no doubt, is that eroticism and expediency had increased and, furthermore, had failed to provide the promised exhilaration and stability.

In the final section of the poem, a voice answers the speaker in the thunder, like the voice answers a knight in the Grail legend. In *The Waste Land*, it answers from the Brihadaranyaka-Upanished: "Datta. Dayadhvam. Damyata." That is, "Give. Sympathize. Control." Kirk writes:

> Give? That means surrender—yielding to something outside one's self. If sexual union is to be fertile, there must occur surrender of self in some degree, momentary self-effacement in another. . . . Sympathize? That means love and loyalty, and the diminishing of private claims. . . . Control? That, as Babbitt had said, is to place restraints upon will and appetite. True control is exerted not through force and a master, but by self-discipline and persuasion of others.

There is no response from the speaker. Kirk writes: "It was painful to seek for those answers; it will be agony to obey. Still the Seeker hesitates, though now the arid plain is behind him. . . . London Bridge is falling down: the outer order of civilization disintegrates. But may not the ruins be shored up? And should not a man commence the work of renewal, spiritual and material, by setting his lands in order: by recovering order within his own soul." "Eliot had asked the great questions," Kirk concludes, "and in *The Waste Land*, here and there, blades of grass had begun to sprout."

Perhaps—though it is worthwhile remembering that Eliot had originally planned to publish *The Waste Land* with "Gerontion" (appearing before it) and "The Hollow Men" (appearing afterwards). How can one give, sympathize, and exercise control when one is a "Paralysed force" and a "gesture without motion," as Eliot put it in "The Hollow Men"? *The Waste Land* ends with an answer—the right answer—but the speaker is unable to enact it. He needs a renewed will. This will not come until "Ash Wednesday" (1930), where the "spirit of the river, spirit of the sea" allows his "cry" to "come unto Thee."

6

The Failure of Surrealism

WHY HAS SURREALISM BEEN such a success in painting and such a failure in poetry? Why do some of the most striking lines in twentieth-century poetry—"the sky flows into their nostrils / like a nutritious blue milk"—go forgotten and unread, if they were ever remembered in the first place? One of the twentieth century's most recognizable images is Salvador Dalí's *The Persistence of Memory*. But if asked to name a single surrealist poem or line of surrealist poetry, most people, critics included, would be stumped.

These were some of the questions that came to mind as I read Willard Bohn's recent anthology, *Surrealist Poetry*. The volume is a bilingual collection of mostly French and Spanish surrealist poetry translated into English. All the big names are here—Louis Aragon, André Breton, René Char, Paul Eluard, Federico García Lorca, and Octavio Paz—as well as a good selection of minor figures like José María Hinojosa and Braulio Arenas.

Surrealism has had an "unprecedented global impact," Bohn writes in the introduction, and he's right about that impact being global, even if it hasn't exactly been unprecedented. It is, without a doubt, the twentieth century's most popular art movement. Unlike cubism or abstract expressionism, it spans all mediums—paint, stone, poetry, and film—and, as a technique for creating images, it has persisted for nearly a hundred years in the work of artists from all continents. The term has even entered everyday discourse. Any situation that is strange or violent, has dreamlike qualities, or evokes a sense of déjà vu is potentially "surreal"—from a *Simpsons* episode to a terrorist attack.

Yet, surrealist poetry "has languished." Why? Bohn says one reason is the lack of English translations, world culture's *lingua franca*. Hence the present volume. But the problem is further up the ladder. There are plenty of translations of Baudelaire and Proust, for example, because so many people think these writers are worth reading and, therefore, worth translating. So why do so few—comparatively, at least—think surrealist poetry is?

Bohn's second reason for surrealist poetry's obscurity is more convincing, though he fails to register the significance of what he is saying. The problem is the medium. The problem is poetry itself. Bohn writes:

> Unlike printed texts, paintings and films offer the illusion of being immediately accessible. Although viewers may have no idea what they really mean, the visual images impinge upon their retinas without need of mediation. The fact that many of the images appear to be realistic, that many objects can actually be identified, reinforces the viewer's impression.

In short, while the images of a surrealist painting are relatively clear (and often enchanting), even if their significance isn't, the same is not true of poetry. Poetic images are constructed with words and syntax within an overarching narrative, if I can use the term loosely, be it discursive, descriptive, or dramatic. Paintings have narratives, too, of course, but they are always created by the images themselves—a gesture suggests a feeling, the light on the eye is a life story. It's nearly the opposite with poetry, whose images work symbiotically within narratives.

Unlike painting's images, the poetic image is revealed *linearly*. One word is encountered after another. Objects take shape by addition. Characters appear. They do things with objects. Speakers speak. These elements must work together in a specific sequence to create, if everything goes right, a complex whole.

The painterly image, however, is revealed in an instant. We might roam the surface, focusing on a detail here, a texture or color there, and relate them back to the whole, but the sequence of that roaming and relating doesn't change the image one bit. Change the sequence of words in a poem, and you have a new poem.

But surrealism doesn't care about narratives. It cares about images. It is an image-making, metaphor-making technique—a way of bringing disparate things together to create a new, strange one. In fact, its disregard for narrative is one of its defining characteristics. It is a form of play, of imagistic exploration.

The Failure of Surrealism

Guillaume Apollinaire certainly had the free play of images in mind when he used the term on May 18, 1917 to describe the ballet *Parade*, for which Picasso had designed the set and costumes (Jean Cocteau wrote the scenario and Erik Satie composed the music). Unlike the "artificial" ("factice") costumes and choreography in most ballets, *Parade* possessed "a sort of sur-realism," Apollinaire wrote. What does he mean?

I don't think it's insignificant that one of Apollinaire's favorite words is "reality." Painters like Picasso, he writes, "are moving further and further away from the old art of optical illusion and local proportions.... *Scientific Cubism* is one of the pure tendencies. It is the art of painting new compositions with elements taken not from reality as it is seen, but from reality as it is known."

Cubism, in other words, is a two-dimensional representation of the mechanics of the mind ("reality as it is known") and it is in this sense, according to Apollinaire, that the flat paintings of cubism are more *realistic* than paintings that use *illusion* to represent how things look. If cubism is a two-dimensional representation of the workings of the mind, *Parade*, with its cubist horses and jesters, may have seemed to Apollinaire a three-dimensional one—a cubist painting in action—and so a "sort of sur-realism."

The other aspect of *Parade* is its childlike play. It brings all the arts together in an expression of "universal jubilation" ("allégresse universelle"). It is both a hard-nosed "translation" of reality and a "free fantasy." The ballet, Apollinaire remarks, "has done something entirely new, marvelously seducing, with a truth so lyrical, humane, and joyful that it will be able to illuminate, if it's worth it, Dürer's terrible black sun in *Adrianeholia*." This last remark suggests, of course, that *Parade* does tell us something (all art does), but Apollinaire is less concerned with this than with the imagistic mingling of reality and fantasy.

André Breton, too, defined surrealism as a play of psychic images. However, for Breton, in the process of this play, a narrative *would* emerge from the images themselves, though, significantly, it would always be the same narrative: a critique of Hegel's idealism, which favored reason over irrationality, "presence" over "absence." Breton writes in his *Second Manifesto* that

> Surrealism, although a special part of its function is to examine with a critical eye the notions of reality and unreality, reason and irrationality, reflection and impulse, knowledge and "fatal"

ignorance, ... tends to take as its point of departure the "colossal abortion" of the Hegelian system.

While still sharing Hegel's method (and so not exactly a critique of Hegel's *system*), surrealism shows, Breton claims, that Hegel's hierarchical distinctions between beauty and ugliness, order and chaos, spirit and matter, are hobgoblins. Everything is one—ugliness is beauty, beauty is ugliness, spirit is matter. So, in place of Hegel's idealism, it proposes a new and supposedly improved dialectic that takes into consideration the *material* ground of being. It is no surprise that Breton would go on to claim that surrealism would prove that "historical materialism" is true.

More could be said about the nuances and contradictions of Breton's definition of surrealism and its relationship to materialism. The point here is that for both Apollinaire and Breton narrative is in no need of the artist's attention. The poet ignores it because it supposedly takes care of itself, emerging ready-made (like form) from a poem's imagery, which is produced, in Breton's view, by some "collective mind." The problem, of course, is that attention to narrative is one of the primary tasks of the poet.

This is why the best poems in *Surrealist Poetry* aren't actually surreal. They ignore Breton's mumbo jumbo about automatic writing (an impossibility, in any case, as Frank O'Hara noted—no writing is ever free of conscious control) while learning from surrealism's advances in metaphor.

The selections from Nobel Prize winner Vicente Aleixandre are particularly instructive. The early surrealist prose poems show the poet's originality and gift for metaphor with lines like "You are the virgin wave of yourself" and "I'll finally hold . . . your demolished torso, twinkling between my teeth," and even these poems have a narrative flow established by mood and voice. But they are inferior to the dialogue poems included in the volume, which are hardly surreal, and which show both Aleixandre's startling vision and narrative craftsmanship. Take "Hands," for example, which begins:

> See your hand, how slowly it moves,
> transparent, tangible, pierced by light,
> lovely, alive, nearly human in the night.
> With the moon's reflection, with a painful cheek, with the
> vagueness of dream. See how it grows when you lift your arm,
> fruitless search for a vanished night,
> wing of light gliding silently
> and brushing against the dark vault.

The Failure of Surrealism

Aleixandre goes on to imagine another hand—figured as a wing—pursuing the first. They "encounter each other" in the sky. They are "signs / calling to each other silently in the dark." In the final stanza, Aleixandre writes, they "collide and cling together igniting / a sudden moon above the world of men."

It's a stunning poem but hardly a surrealist one. Bohn may have included it, and other dialogue poems by Aleixandre, because of its other-worldly final image—the hands joining together to form a moon—or because of the specter of death that haunts the poem. (The hands are described at one point to be those of "lovers recently deceased.") But those elements are hardly exclusive to surrealism. The "fantastic" has a long history in poetry.

Neither does the poem disregard narrative or randomly join disparate images. In fact, like the French poet Yves Bonnefoy, who also toyed with surrealism in his early work, Aleixandre returns again and again to the image of hands (as well as stones and light) in his work. This is a conscious preoccupation not an unconscious one.

Compare Aleixandre's poem to another that has hands: Louis Aragon's "Drinking Song." The poem begins beautifully and surprisingly with a comparison of water glasses to zeppelins and hands to birds:

> If water glasses were really water glasses
> And not airships
> Sailing at night toward painted lips
> Hands would still be birds

But after this, it's as if Aragon gives up:

> Hands that close on alcohol
> Hands that hug the fire-damp
> The sheep grazing on the tablecloth
> Do not fear the doves because
> Of their whiteness
> Let me laugh
>
> Doves you not only threaten
> The observation balloon that resembles me
> Like a brother but
> Also the leaden plain

The Soul Is a Stranger in This World

> Look look how the hands I love
> In the morning when the illuminated signs
> Still rival the dawn how
> They bend the sheep's spines
> Crack vertebrae
> Ah ah the silver-plate was false
> The spoons are made of lead like bullets

The sudden shift of vision (from hands to sheep) and voice ("Let me laugh"), aborting the initial metaphors, empties the comparisons of potential significance. While Aragon maintains some continuity—the hands becomes doves that "bend the sheep's spines"—the metaphor ultimately tells us very little about human love or violence. It is made flat by the poem's disregard for narrative.

Breton held that the practice of automatic writing would produce images of great beauty and reality. They would "enrapture" the mind, he wrote, revealing the foundational truths of the human psyche and the world:

> [T]he Surrealist atmosphere created by automatic writing, which I have wanted to put within reach of everyone, is especially conducive to the production of beautiful images. One can even go so far as to say that in this dizzying race the images appear like the only guideposts of the mind. By slow degrees the mind becomes convinced of the supreme reality of these images.

But if there's one thing that surrealist poetry doesn't do, it is convince us of the "supreme reality" of its images. In fact, as *Surrealist Poetry* shows, while surrealism's metaphors can dazzle, they are most forgettable precisely because they tell us so little. An "elevator cage" is "bursting with tufts of / women's lingerie," a "wolf with glass teeth . . . eats up time in little round cans," space yields "its full mental cotton," ladies bolt "their metaphysical doors," a woman is "the present that accumulates second by second," and on, and on. The volume is full of such images, but it is often unclear what they might mean without the context of narrative, which makes them mere confections—hardly the hard-nosed philosophical aesthetic Breton championed.

The result is boredom. I could look at Max Ernst's drawings in *Histoire Naturelle* (1926) for hours, but reading even the best "absolute" surrealist poem is something like 10 percent exhilaration and 90 percent standing in line at the DMV.

The Failure of Surrealism

Does this mean surrealist poetry isn't worth reading? No, there is a real benefit to poets and writers in studying surrealism's experiments in metaphor while moving on, as most of the poets in this volume did, once the lessons have been learned. But there are fewer benefits for the general reader. It is an intriguing theory of image-making, but a limited theory of art, and because of this, it regularly fails to please—the first criterion of great art.

7

WWI Poets Reconsidered

BRITISH POETS OF WORLD War I are often thought of as antiwar because of the horror and suffering rendered in their work. Wilfred Owen's "Dulce et Decorum Est," for instance, describes a gas attack in gruesome detail and ends with the following famous admonition:

> My friend, you would not tell with
> such high zest
>
> To children ardent for some
> desperate glory,
>
> The old Lie: Dulce et decorum est
>
> Pro patria mori.

Because Owen's poems regularly show that it need not be either "sweet" or "proper" to die for one's country, his work and name are occasionally used in support of pacifist causes. Composer and conscientious objector Benjamin Britten set his 1962 "War Requiem" to Owen's poems, and in 2005 playwright Harold Pinter claimed that Owen would have shared "our contempt, our revulsion, our nausea" at the war in Iraq.

But Owen was no pacifist. Not only did he die in battle, in November 1918, he earned a Military Cross for inflicting "considerable losses on the enemy" and believed that the war was a necessary evil. In June 1917, he wrote his mother that the "Aim in War" was the "Extinction of Militarism, beginning with Prussian." In September 1917, he wrote: "I hate washy pacifists as temperamentally as I hate whiskied prussianists."

Some Desperate Glory, which takes its title from Owen's poem, is a mix of narrative, portraiture, and selections of poetry from British soldiers during World War I. Max Egremont's choices demonstrate that, while the poems generally became less idealistic as the war progressed, many poets continued to believe in the necessity of opposing German expansionism.

The first section of Egremont's volume focuses mainly on Rupert Brooke, who became the early voice of the war. Brooke was the first of the soldier-poets to see action. He joined the Royal Navy Division on Sept. 27, 1914, and left for Antwerp via France on Oct. 4 to help defend the city against German advances. It was there that Brooke first experienced what he called "the incessant mechanical slaughter of . . . modern battles." The German siege had created "hundreds of thousands of refugees," Brooke wrote in a letter, "their goods on barrows and hand-carts, . . . the old men mostly weeping, the women with hard drawn faces, the children playing or crying or sleeping. That's what Belgium is now: the country where three civilians have been killed for every one soldier."

The horror of German shelling and the high civilian casualty in Belgium, however, convinced Brooke of the necessity of British involvement. In the sonnets that he wrote upon his return from Belgium, he praised the sacrifice of British soldiers, who in death became "rarer gifts than gold." He even expressed hope that the war might be a form of moral (and perhaps artistic) cleansing. "God be thanked," he wrote in "Peace," "Who has matched us with His hour, . . . / With hand made sure, clear eye, and sharpened power, / To turn, as swimmers into cleanness leaping."

Brooke was not alone in viewing the war in such terms. Julian Grenfell, who enlisted, like Siegfried Sassoon, seeking adventure, wrote in "Into Battle" that "he is dead who will not fight; / And who dies fighting has increase." In "To the Poet Before Battle," Ivor Gurney tells his fellow poets to "make / The name of poet terrible in just war," and in "Battery Moving Up to a New Position," Robert Nichols compares British soldiers to Christ, as they take a position on "our Golgotha, to make / For all our lovers sacrifice."

Furthermore, as Egremont's selections show, the move from idealism to realism was hardly uniform. Sassoon, who in 1917 would briefly lend his support to the pacifist cause, wrote in 1915 that "war has made us wise, / And, fighting for our freedom, we are free." In 1916, Sassoon, angered at the death of his friend David Thomas, addresses his gun in "The Kiss":

> To these I turn, in these I trust—
> Brother Lead and Sister Steel.
> To his blind power I make appeal,
> I guard her beauty clean from rust.
> He spins and burns and loves the air,
> And splits a skull to win my praise.

Yet, that same year, Sassoon complained about war's injustice in "The Death Bed" while lamenting the death of one his comrades: "He's young; he hated War; how should he die / When cruel old campaigners win safe through?"

One of the most frequent complaints of the soldier-poets was against the inexperience and disorganization of the British command. In "Servitude," Ivor Gurney writes: "If it were not for England, who would bear / This heavy servitude one moment more? . . . Harried in foolishness, scanned curiously o'er / By fools made brazen by conceit." In "The General," Sassoon lambastes the general's happy ignorance and seethes at the "incompetent swine" who pass for his staff.

Many poets loathed the war for its brutality and pushed back against the demonization of the Germans. In "This Is No Case of Petty Right or Wrong," Edward Thomas wrote famously: "I hate not Germans, nor grow hot / With love of Englishmen, to please newspapers," and Charles Sorley expressed hope in "To Germany" that "When it is peace, then we may view again / With new-won eyes each other's truer form."

While the war didn't create any Homeric epics, Tim Kendall's *Poetry of the First World War*, an anthology with helpful, unobtrusive editorial notes on the poems, shows how it transformed occasional writers into poets who wrote some of the generation's most moving poems. Edward Thomas considered himself a "doomed hack" before the war but found his voice in poems like "In Memoriam" and "The Cherry Trees." And the war gave Edmund Blunden, who thought of himself as "a harmless young shepherd in a soldier's coat," a subject ironically suited to his pastoral gifts. In a poem on Thievpal Wood during the battle of the Somme, Blunden writes that "shell-fountains leap from the swamps" and "Ember-black the gibbet trees like bones or thorns protrude."

The mixing of the pastoral and the gruesome is one of the central characteristics of British war poetry and one that it shares with the *Iliad*. "I saw his round mouth's crimson deepen as it fell, / Like a sun, in his last deep hour," Wilfred Owen writes in an untitled poem. In "A Night Attack,"

Siegfried Sassoon describes the front line as "Brown lines of tents are hives for snoring men; / Wide, radiant water sways the floating sky."

The idea that one of Britain's greatest achievements was its literature was widespread at the time. This was a period, Kendall notes, when British poets were moving away from the "florid late-Victorian rhetoric" and toward a simple diction and "tonal restraint" that characterized Georgian poetry. This proved particularly well suited for capturing the horrors of mass mechanical warfare. And a few poets, such as Isaac Rosenberg and David Jones, found freedom in the trenches to be more formally experimental.

Kendall's volume contains poems by Rosenberg, whose restrained, sonorous compound nouns and regular juxtaposition of the spiritual and the profane caught the attention of Ezra Pound. There is also a section of Jones's 1937 experimental masterpiece, "In Parenthesis," which the poet called "a shape in words" and which T. S. Eliot praised as "a work of genius."

More writers and poets fought in World War I than in any other British war. Of those included in Kendall's anthology, half died during the war. The survivors and civilians were hardly luckier. May Wedderburn Cannan hoped that after the war she might sit with her fiancé on a terrace "and see the changeless sky and hills beat blue / And live an afternoon of summer through," but she would be disappointed. Her fiancé died of the flu while traveling with his unit in 1919. We, on the other hand, can and often do live such afternoons. Both *Some Desperate Glory* and *Poetry of the First World War* are reminders of war's great cost and occasional necessity.

8

Fancy and Faith in Wallace Stevens

WITH LINES LIKE "CALL the roller of big cigars / The muscular one, and bid him whip / In kitchen cups concupiscent curds," Wallace Stevens's *Harmonium* (1923) should have announced the arrival of a new talent. It didn't. Published a month before the poet's forty-fourth birthday, the book provoked mostly lukewarm reviews, and what interest the volume may have garnered evaporated in time as readers turned their attention to a still young T. S. Eliot, the expatriate whose *The Waste Land*, published at the end of 1922, hit readers, as the poet William Carlos Williams would later put it, like "an atom bomb."

In Paul Mariani's biography of the poet, *The Whole Harmonium*, Stevens seems barely to register the apparent failure, though he soon after took his longest break ever from writing. A month after *Harmonium* appeared, he left with his wife, Elsie, for a proper honeymoon—something he had postponed for more than a decade—and spent the better part of the following six years working quietly in his job as a corporate executive and watching a daughter, who was born in 1924, grow. In 1928, Williams complained in a note to Pound: "Undecipherable letter from Wallace Stevens. He says he isn't writing any more. He has a daughter!" This could have marked the end of a poetic career that was already characterized by fits and starts.

Born in Reading, Pennsylvania, Stevens went by "Pat" at school and ran around with the town hooligans, playing poker and pool, before a bout of malaria caused him to have to repeat the ninth grade. When he returned to Reading Boys' High School that fall, he was a changed youth—singing in the church choir, reading Poe and Hawthorne at night, and throwing himself into his studies with a new seriousness while still playing left end for the football team. He became editor of the school paper and graduated near the top of his class in 1897, giving the school's valedictorian address.

Completing Harvard in three years instead of four, and taking courses in English and philosophy, he filled his university journals with sonnets on the "monstrous pleasure" of "unexpected, commonplace, specific things," like a drop of rain on a leaf or the "thin whiteness" of a sunset. Some of these he published in the *Harvard Advocate*, of which he would become president in his final semester. After he left Harvard in 1900, he did not publish a poem for another fourteen years. By the time he was thirty-four, he had tried and given up on a career in journalism, graduated from law school, and had just been hired as the vice president of the New York office of a St. Louis insurance firm.

Stevens's dream of becoming a poet was back in the cards by 1914, however, when five poems appeared in the magazine *Trend*. Within a year, he was eating with Marcel Duchamp at night while maintaining a busy work schedule and keeping up appearances at home. When the poet and art collector Walter Arensberg met Stevens around this time, he called him a "rogue elephant in porcelain"—smooth refinement on the outside but brooding independence and a single-minded dedication to his craft on the inside. These would carry him past the initial dismissal of *Harmonium* by critics. He went on to publish *Ideas of Order* in 1936 and *The Auroras of Autumn* in 1950, among other volumes. They would slowly establish him as a master of metaphor and one of the twentieth century's pre-eminent poets.

As incongruous as Stevens's life might sound initially (he was a conservative insurance executive and a modernist poet who once got into a fistfight with Ernest Hemingway), what mattered most to Stevens was poetry's power to capture the "Passions of rain" and subdue the "unsubdued / Elations when the forest blooms." He hoped to give language a richness and density and to give the quotidian a strangely evocative newness—a philosophical weight.

"Life is an affair of people not of places," he once wrote. "But for me life is an affair of places and that is the trouble." This may sound odd coming from a poet who lived in Hartford, Connecticut, for nearly forty years and who—unlike so many modern American poets—never left the continent. But it's largely true if we take "places" to mean not just his childhood home in Reading or his February trips to Key West, Florida, but the "dwelling" that the mind makes out of nature.

For Stevens, nature may be the result of an impersonal force—thus, little more than the "meaningless plunging of water and the wind"—but when transformed by the imagination it could become a "deepening, enchanting night." Stevens's question was how to account for the imagination without invoking a God that he regarded for most of his life as "the last distortion of romance."

His first collection, *Harmonium*, is both playful and sonorous, full of life's colors, sounds, and bric-a-brac, while also seeming to cast a cold eye on the comforts of religion. Life is a "bawdiness, / Unpurged by epitaph, indulged at last." The only comfort in death, Stevens writes in "Peter Quince at the Clavier," is in knowing that the music of the poet's "bawdy strings" might sound "a constant sacrament of praise."

The way that sound shapes poetry has generally become less evident as poets have discarded regular meter and end rhyme, turning to typography or formal devices such as the arbitrary constraints of technology to shape poems. But regular meter and end rhyme are not the only sources of sound in poetry. Repetition of words or phrases, assonance, alliteration, internal rhyme, pauses created by line spacing of punctuation or even diction all contribute to the length and pace of the lines and stanzas of a poem. "You have somehow to know the sound that is the exact sound," Stevens once remarked, "and you do in fact know, without knowing how." The "exact" sound for Stevens is that phoneme that has just the right variation with respect to the rest of the sounds in the poem to produce (coupled with the meaning of the word) a moment of "exhilaration."

In his famous poem "Delight in Disorder" (1648), Robert Herrick associates the surprise of variation in poetry with the errant ribbons and suggestively untied shoe strings (!) in the dress of a beautiful woman. He concludes that such "distractions" "do more bewitch me than when art / is too precise in every part." Herrick playfully suggests that variation is an expression of "wantonness," and, of course, it can be when it is a perversion that undermines rather than adds to the nuance and complexity of the order of things.

But Stevens, like most poets, sees something else in the pleasure of variation. In a 1935 letter (Frank Doggett reminds us in *Wallace Stevens: The Making of the Poem*), Stevens wrote that he found "most attractive" the idea that "we are all the merest biological mechanisms," remarking that a poem embodies the complex mechanisms of the universe. This idea is expressed in the first stanza of "The Idea of Order at Key West" in the sea's "mimic motion" that both "made constant cry" and "caused constantly a cry."

At the same time, Stevens believed that a poem also transforms the material world by an agency (the imagination) that is both part of and distinct from matter. We see this in the opening line of the poem and in the second stanza. The voice sings "beyond" the sea. It is distinct from the sea's sound but indebted in some way to the sea's "genius," its originality, for its own originality (and embodied in the irregular alliteration). The sea, in turn, becomes the self that is the song of the woman, without which it is simply "grinding water and the gasping wind." The woman's transformation of the sea by varying its unchanging "inhuman" repetition creates a moment of "exhilaration" for her audience: "It was her voice," Stevens writes, that made the "sky acutest at its vanishing."

Variation points us to a creative force or agent distinct from the material world—a great "Comedian" or, as Stevens suggested in his letters and essays, a collective unconscious or "infinite extension of personality." Or one could simply follow Gerard Manley Hopkins, who says what Stevens was unwilling to say: that variation points to God himself, the great poetic "I am." This may have been what Stevens did.

He would become ambivalent about the *Harmonium*'s word play—claiming in 1935 that when he composed *Harmonium* he "liked the idea of images and images alone. . . . But we live in a different time." Four years later, he told the editor of the French translation of *Harmonium* that "my own way out toward the future involves a confidence in the spiritual role of the poet . . . in restoring to the imagination what it is losing at such a catastrophic pace."

What our shared imagination was losing seems to have been a belief in the essential goodness of order and the pleasure it produces. Later, Stevens would express disgust at the chaos of increasingly surrealistic art, which seemed to value novelty and freedom above all else. While Stevens argues in "The Idea of Order at Key West" that there is no world except the one that we (or the poets) create in our imagination, he would also argue in his lecture "The Irrational Element in Poetry" at Harvard that same year that poetry was an attempt to find the good—"the harmonious and orderly," as he called it—"which, in the Platonic sense, is synonymous with God." By 1951, Stevens was claiming that "God and the imagination are one."

Is this equation of God and the imagination an expression of Stevens's final faith in poetry or his evolving understanding of a central but nontraditional deity, or both? It's hard to say. Stevens was reading a New Testament at St. Francis Hospital in Hartford, where he had chosen to be admitted shortly before his death in 1955. (He had thrown his childhood Bible away almost fifty years earlier.) He told the chaplain, the Rev. Arthur Hanley, that what bothered him was "how a just God could construct a place like hell." A few days before his death, he asked to be baptized into the Roman Catholic Church.

9

Robert Frost's Women and Men

ROBERT FROST HAS OFTEN been the object of two wildly conflicting critiques—that he was an egotistical man who cared little for "everyday" people and that he cared about such people too much. In a recent story published in *Harper's*, for example, Joyce Carol Oates imagines what it would have been like for an elderly Robert Frost—fat and drooling—to be interviewed by a young, female college student on his front porch in 1951. The student adores Frost at first, but as she speaks with him, she discovers that he is a misogynistic pervert who prefers fawning adoration to intelligent dialogue.

Midway through the story, after rejecting Frost's unwanted advances, she turns on the poet and berates him for nearly two pages for his unenlightened attitude towards women and his bigotry towards nonwhites. In one passage, she tells Frost that "The Gift Outright" seems "to endorse manifest destiny" and "totally excludes native Americans"—"the numerous tribes of Indians," she explains, in case the poet had not heard of a term that would not be widely used until twenty years after his death, "who lived in North America long before the European settlers arrived." Of course, Frost is unable to withstand such blistering intelligence. He stammers as he flees the porch and falls into the mud. *Fin.*

It's a piece of fiction, of course, and not a very good one; but Joyce Carol Oates suggests that the portrait is at least partly true when she notes that it is "based on (limited, selected) historical research" and cites Jeffrey Meyers's 1996 biography of the poet as a source. Of course, Meyers's biography draws heavily from Lawrance Thompson's biased portrait of Frost as a self-absorbed, vindictive ogre; but while Thompson's treatment of Frost has been debunked by William H. Pritchard, Jay Parini, and others, the image of Frost as a "monster of egotism" (as Helen Vendler put it) remains in certain circles—and surfaces from time to time, such as in Oates's story.

Frost's letters strike another blow against Lawrance Thompson's biased portrait. Like most artists and other men of talent, Frost had a high view of his work. In an early letter, he tells his friend and former student John Bartlett that he is "one of the few artists writing." He touts the success of his first two books of poems to American publishers and friends. (Frost published both *A Boy's Will* and *North of Boston* in England with David Nutt and Company, in 1913 and 1914, respectively.) *North of Boston* is "epoch making," he writes in one letter, and he boasts in another that reviews of the book "have all been ridiculously favorable."

But this early tub-thumping disappears as Frost begins to gain a wider audience. "I'm rather pleased to have attained to a position," he confesses to Edwin Arlington Robinson in 1915, "where I don't have to admire my work as much as I had to when no one else admired it." Overall, the letters show Frost to be a mature artist, a good friend, and a caring husband and father.

While the volume contains a few boyhood letters, the majority of the correspondence here is from 1912 to 1920. Frost married Elinor White in 1895, and for nearly twenty years, he wrote poetry in the evenings while variously farming, studying at Harvard, and working as a journalist and teacher. In 1912, the Frosts moved to England with their four children; there, he devoted himself to writing full-time. Until then, Frost had only published a handful of poems in small New York and Boston magazines. But his two years in England would mark the beginning of a long, successful poetic career.

Of course, Frost was no saint; but these letters nevertheless show him to be a faithful friend, a good husband, and a caring father. He certainly was not a misogynist. He was deeply concerned for Elinor after she had a miscarriage in 1915, and he complained to Louis Untermeyer about Amy Lowell's description of his wife in an essay about him. Frost was angered that Lowell made Elinor out to be "the conventional helpmeet of genius":

> Catch her getting any satisfaction out of what her housekeeping may have done to feed a poet! Rats! She hates housekeeping. She has worked because the work has piled on top of her. But she hasn't pretended to like housework even for my sake. If she has liked anything it has been what I may call living it on the high. She's especially wary of honors that derogate from the poetic life she

fancies us living. What a cheap common unindividualized picture Amy makes of her.

He dotes on his first daughter, Lesley, and writes her long, encouraging, fatherly letters while she is away at college.

This image of Frost as a loving husband and doting father is confirmed in his granddaughter's *You Come Too: My Journey with Robert Frost*, part memoir, part thematic biography focusing on Frost's relationship with women. In it, Lesley Lee Francis recounts her mother's memory (also Lesley) of her father and her own interaction with him as his granddaughter.

The early years were not always easy. The children (there were four of them by 1905) were schooled at home, and while Frost farmed and later taught at Pinkerton Academy, he was also heavily involved in their education, teaching them botany and astronomy, writing stories and poems for them, and responding to their writing.

Frost's daughter's journals, which Francis quotes extensively, show a healthy, active family in which the daily lives of parents and children were tightly interwoven. Not only did Frost ask his children to type clean copies of his poems, but as many as thirty of his early poems treated topics that his children also wrote about in their compositions. This suggests that these topics were part of a larger family conversation.

As Francis shows, family life was important to Frost's work. While his poems are very much for adults and both playful and dark, which Francis too often ignores, she's right to note the importance of children as characters in his work. Frost once remarked to Cleanth Brooks and Robert Penn Warren that he wanted to throw readers "back on their Mother Goose . . . with the play of ideas in it; how deep Mother Goose is."

When Lesley went to Wellesley College, Frost's letters to her show him to have been a patient, supportive, and occasionally worried father, particularly after she had failed to make the tennis team. He encourages her to spend her money wisely and tells her, though Francis does not mention this exchange, to "Keep your balance—that's all. Your marks don't matter."

Many of these anecdotes of the Frosts' early years were treated (some verbatim) in Francis's earlier volume, *Robert Frost: An Adventure in Poetry, 1900–1918*. In *You Come Too*, however, she also looks at her grandfather's relationship with his wife and his eldest daughter, Lesley, after 1918 and his relationship with three women outside the family who played an important role in his life as a poet—Susan Hayes Ward, Harriet Monroe, and the poet Amy Lowell.

Susan Hayes Ward, literary editor of the New York *Independent*, published Frost's "My Butterfly: An Elegy," which started a correspondence and eventually friendship between the older Ward, her clergyman brother, and the younger Frosts. Ward was pivotal in encouraging the young poet. Frost's correspondence with Marianne Monroe, the founder and editor of *Poetry*, and Lowell was at times good-naturedly combative on matters of prosody, yet it was through such interactions that Frost came to develop his ideas about what he called the "sound of sense," which he first mentioned in a letter to John Bartlett while he was living in England.

In all of these relationships, Elinor was an equal party, frequently writing letters to both Monroe and Lowell, and participating in visits and discussions when she could, though obviously limited by the responsibilities of child-rearing. Frost loved Elinor, and Elinor was deeply committed to Frost's poetry and willing to make whatever sacrifices were necessary for him to pursue it, even if she disliked the fame it brought. She was his first and most important critic—"the unspoken half of everything I ever wrote," Frost once told his friends, "and both halves of many a thing." So, no, Joyce Carole Oates, Frost was neither a misanthrope nor a misogynist.

The other critique of Frost—that he cared for everyday people too much and took them too seriously in his work—was perhaps put most strongly by Yvor Winters, the now largely forgotten modernist poet and critic. In 1948, he wrote that while Frost is sometimes "praised as a classical poet," he is, in fact no such thing. Classical literature glorifies noble characters, Winters wrote, while Frost's poetry glorifies the "average" human being. "The human average has never been admirable," Winters continued, "and that is why literature which glorifies the average is sentimental." Frost is "a poet of the minor theme, the casual approach, and the discreetly eccentric attitude."

Winters was not the first to characterize Frost as a simple, folksy poet who retreated from the modern world to the New England countryside. In 1936, William Rose Benét called Frost a "wise old woodchuck." That is, Frost "is a close observer of the earth and the ways of man on the earth." Yet to call Frost a "woodchuck"—one of the Northeast's most common mammals—is to present him, wittingly or unwittingly, as a regional poet. Writing a few years earlier, Frederic Carpenter states, rather bluntly, that Frost lacks the "cosmic imagination" and "power" of Whitman. He has limited his poems to the occasional subject, the personal tenor, and everyday mankind, "renouncing the possibility of becoming something greater."

In *The Art of Robert Frost*, however, Tim Kendall sees in Frost a trait common to all great artists: the ability, as Frost himself put it, "to be a poet for all sorts and kinds." Frost's best poems, according to Kendall, have at least two meanings—a "particular" and an "ulterior" one. This may be true of all art, but great artists are those whose "particular" meaning is expressed so well that readers, as Frost is reported to have said, "might feel free to settle for that part of the poem as sufficient in itself."

Too many readers have settled for the well-said particular meaning of Frost's poems, reducing him to a mere nature poet. Yet, there is a tension in his work between "the world," which almost always means "civilization" for Frost, and nature. The latter does not always offer a respite from the evils of the former. In "Into My Own," one of Frost's earliest poems, a youth "Fearless of ever finding open land" is persuaded, according to Frost's authorial note, "that he will be rather more than less himself for having foresworn the world." "Freedom," Frost wrote in 1959, "is nothing but departure—setting forth—leaving things behind, brave origination of the courage to be new," and it's for freedom that the youth in "Into My Own" determines to "steal away" into the vast "dark trees." The result, the youth imagines, will be self-realization:

> I do not see why I should e'er turn back,
> Or those should not set forth upon my track
> To overtake me, who should miss me here
> And long to know if still I held them dear.
> They would not find me changed from him they knew—
> Only more sure of all I thought was true.

There is no regret or loss here, only a hypothetical increase in surety of all the youth "thought was true" that is simultaneously admirable and sadly obstinate. (Frost once told the poet Edward Thomas, in his own sadly obstinate moment, "I dont [sic] suppose I was ever sorry for anything I ever did except by assumption to see how it would feel." "Regret," Kendall writes, "in Frost's view, is a self-indulgent emotion which does nothing to assist those who have been wronged.")

Yet, as Kendall points out, this rejection of human society, which the youth imagines will bring a personal expansion, is questioned in Frost's other works. In "The Tuft of Flowers," which was also first printed in *A Boy's Will*, a mower working alone discovers "a tall tuft of flowers beside a brook" that the previous day's mower had left. The flowers draw the two mowers together: "As a consequence, the 'one whose thought I had not hoped to reach' can now be addressed in 'brotherly speech' and treated as 'a spirit kindred to my own.'" The loneliness that the mower had earlier felt is extinguished by the community provided in work.

In *North of Boston*, Frost's second collection, the importance of community is announced in the first poem, "The Pasture," in which the poet invites us to come with him as he goes to "clean the pasture spring" and "fetch the little calf." Kendall observes that this opening piece not only shows Frost's classical knowledge—"Just as Greek antiquity associated the Muses with springs, so Frost locates and tends the pastoral source of his poetic inspiration in his own 'pasture spring'"—it also "prefigures a group of poems concerned with the interplay of open and closed spaces, with windows and doorways, with walls built and breached, and with barriers between people." Regarding the latter, Kendall has in mind poems where walls built out of ignorance ("Mending Wall") or tragedy ("Home Burial") drive people apart.

In all of these poems, Frost's ulterior meaning is often missed because readers fail to follow subtle clues. "The Tuft of Flowers," for example, can be reduced to the final pat lines of the poem, "Men work together . . . /Whether they work together or apart." Yet, as Kendall notes, the flowers symbolize art in the absence of utilitarian value and in the community they create. The poem also comments on how artists work. The first mower, Frost writes, had left the flowers "not for us, / Nor yet to draw one thought of ours to him. /But from sheer morning gladness at the brim."

He was, in other words, an artist, creating beautiful objects—ironically depicted here as *not* cutting the flowers, a minimalist act that beats even Duchamp's signing of his "Fountain"—neither for others nor for personal fame but for the pleasure found in beauty alone. The second mower, also an artist, continues the first's work, building on the foundation before him and experiencing the communion of his absent yet present co-laborer.

This may have been why it was important for Frost to be read by American readers. It is significant that it was in his letters while he was living in England that he first remarked that "nothing is quite honest that is not commercial." Frost mentions this twice. The first time, he immediately adds, "I don't put it that everything commercial is honest." A few days later, Frost explains that commercial success is a sign that his poetry is "honest," because men are willing to work and pay for it. "Nothing is true," he writes, "except as a man or men adhere to it—to live for it, spend themselves on it."

Frost didn't write *for* his audience exactly. He was no country bumpkin, as he sometimes affected. He worried about being "ruined" by his audience. "I am made too self-conscious by the comment on my first book to think of showing another like it for some time," he confessed. But he did want to be widely read by "all sorts and kinds" of people, because that would mean that what he had written was art, not just confection.

The larger context of these remarks, interestingly enough, is Frost's feud with Ezra Pound. Frost first met Pound in 1913, and though the two poets were friends at first, the relationship quickly soured. Pound lauded *A Boy's Will*, but Frost became concerned that Pound would ruin his opportunities with an American audience by making him out to be another expatriate artist rejected by his own country. "Nothing could be more unfair," Frost writes, "nothing better calculated to make me an exile for life."

Frost wanted to reach a wide, particularly American, audience with his poetry. "I could never make a merit of being caviar to the crowd the way my quasi-friend Pound does," he writes. "I want to reach out." Frost saw Pound's poetry as superficially elitist and occasionally needled Pound for his pretension. "Someone says," Frost writes with evident delight, "he looks altogether too much like a poet to be a poet." While Pound would go on to call Frost "a bloated capitalist," Frost was somewhat more long-suffering, ignoring the comment and Pound from that moment on.

10

Cummings's Ear

E. E. CUMMINGS WAS A Harvard man who lived a mostly bohemian life in Greenwich until his death in 1962. His big idea was freedom—both in art and life—yet for all his experiments with typography and punctuation, he was deeply indebted to traditional poetic forms, particularly the sonnet. He believed in a divine power but had no time for religion. He hated communism and the New Deal, loved sex and Paris, and was a staunch supporter of McCarthyism.

He was born in Cambridge, Massachusetts, to upper-middle-class parents. His father was a Unitarian minister and a professor at Harvard. His mother, Susan Cheever writes in a recent biography, "was the aristocrat of the family; her forebears . . . had been distinguished Unitarian writers, judges, and adventurers." She was also, it seems, the perfect mother, loving Cummings "to the fullest measure."

The Cummings household was relatively relaxed. "Children came over to play on the swings and in a sandbox," Cheever writes, "and in a tree house built for their delight in spaces that, in neighboring houses, might have been groomed and manicured." The family spent summers in New Hampshire on Silver Lake, where Cummings would run free with his faithful dog, Rex.

Cummings began Harvard at sixteen in 1911, but he continued to live with his parents until he moved into a dormitory in Harvard Yard for his senior year. All of a sudden, it seems, he became a sex-obsessed, angry, rebellious provocateur. "His behavior changed," Cheever writes, "from that of a rule follower and believer in the Unitarian Church and all its puritanical precepts, as embodied in his powerful, hulking father, to being a trickster."

How did this happen? As Cheever tells it, Cummings's childhood was idyllic except for two events. The first was watching "two smooth cows being driven to the slaughterhouse"—an example of the neighborhood's "dark side," according to Cheever. The second was the drowning of his dog, Rex. Cummings, his sister, and the dog turned over in a canoe on Silver Lake far from shore. The dog panicked and began climbing first on Cummings's sister, then on Cummings. In order to save himself and his sister, the young Cummings held Rex under water until he stopped struggling, left the dog and swam to shore.

The rebelliousness that suddenly surged to the surface in his senior year at Harvard, Cheever speculates, was rooted in the drowning of his dog and resentment against his too-perfect father: "His experiences as a boy, after the death of Rex and with his overwhelmingly excellent father, may have laid the groundwork for his anger." That Cummings's rebellion had anything to do with the drowning of his dog is wildly unlikely, but it certainly had something to do with his father's preoccupation with social issues and unwavering high moral principles, as Christopher Sawyer-Laucanno notes in what is still the definitive biography. "My father," Cummings wrote, "was a walking Platonic triad—the good, the true, the beautiful." Because Cummings felt he could not match his father's goodness, so this reading of his life goes, he chose a different path.

It could also be that Cummings was simply spoiled. His parents doted on him, and his mother hoped that Cummings would one day become a great poet. During his freshman year at Harvard, Cummings wrote, "I am of the aristocracy of this earth. . . . All the advantages that any boy should have are in my hands. I am a king over my opportunities." What may have been the cute playfulness of a somewhat self-absorbed boy developed into something not so cute as he grew older.

Much of Cummings's life would be marked by a sort of selfishness. After Harvard, he worked for three months in the shipping department of the Collier publishing house—his first and last full-time job—and joined a private ambulance corps to avoid being forcibly enlisted. He and another volunteer were held up in Paris because of a bureaucratic hitch. When Cummings finally arrived at the front five weeks later, he seemed to view the whole experience as a game, angering French soldiers, his fellow volunteers, and those in charge. Cummings was arrested as a possible traitor.

And while he was not convicted, he spent three months in a large holding cell, which was the topic of his prose work *The Enormous Room*.

When he returned from his three-month imprisonment, Cummings took up with Elaine Eliot, the wife of his friend Scofield Thayer, the wealthy benefactor of *Dial* magazine. Cummings and Elaine would marry shortly after she and Thayer divorced. The marriage was short and unhappy. Elaine seemed to want a traditional relationship, but Cummings was too often inattentive. When her sister died of pneumonia, the event hardly registered for Cummings. Cheever writes:

> An old-fashioned husband would have been on hand to help with the legal and emotional complications of such an intimate loss.... Cummings, however, was the new kind of husband, and he hardly paid attention. Cummings may have had an *idée fixe* of right and wrong, but when it came to managing the adult world with all its aggravations and necessities, he was useless.

Cummings married a second time, which ended badly, but eventually found a loving and reliable (if not always faithful) partner in the tall, beautiful Marion Morehouse, with whom he would live for the rest of his life.

While Cummings was largely uninterested in politics early in his life, this changed when he visited Russia in 1931. His friends had given glowing reports of the revolution, and Cummings himself was sympathetic to any person or persons who had thrown off the shackles of authority. But Russia was not what Cummings had expected. Instead of freedom, he found oppression, fear, and hypocrisy. It disgusted him.

Never one to back away from a fight, Cummings eviscerated the Russian experiment in *Eimi*, a novelistic memoir that takes Dante's *Inferno* as its example. His friends in Greenwich were not impressed, and Cummings, who had never had a problem publishing, temporarily found it difficult to place his work. But the publication of his *Collected Poems* in 1938—an idea suggested by his agent since much of his work was out of print—changed everything. It was a success with critics and readers alike and was shortlisted for a Pulitzer. "Cummings," Cheever writes, "was hailed as an important poet." Cummings continued to write, and his reputation continued to grow. He reunited briefly with his daughter and took up a lucrative but demanding schedule of readings during the last ten years of his life.

While he is remembered for his use of lower-case letters and nonstandard punctuation and for his biting satires, Cheever reminds us that Cummings was also a gifted lyricist who was often preoccupied with nature: "i thank You God," Cummings writes, "for most this amazing / day: for the leaping greenly spirits of trees / and a blue true dream of sky; and for everything / which is natural which is infinite which is yes."

R. P. Blackmur's remark that Cummings's poetry is "a kind of baby-talk" is not quite fair, though Cummings could definitely be both infantile and cruel. In his early volumes, he describes prostitutes and his own lusty feelings with the precision and imagination of a schoolboy. In "Gert," for example, he writes "joggle i think will do it although the glad / monosyllable jounce possibly can tell / better how the balloons move." "Her voice? / gruesome: a trull / leaps from the lungs 'gimme uh swell fite . . . .'" Sometimes he doesn't even bother to name the women because all he sees is body parts—like a "huge dropping of a flesh from / hinging thighs" and a "small manure-shaped head" on a pillow. For "two dollars," he says he will a woman's "hips with boys and girls." He confesses that he likes "best,the,stomachs,of the young (girls silky and lewd)," but he's also happy with "electric trite / thighs," lips, or any "curve of flesh." Women are inanimate objects or events. A girl is "a leaf," a woman is "the wind" or "like / the rain."

When he's not lusty, he can be angry—at "humanity," at the war, at the stupidity of the "clean upstanding well dressed" boys, at the ladies of Cambridge, Massachusetts. "Humanity i love you," he writes in "La Guerre," but he doesn't, as becomes clear in the next line: "because you would rather black the boots of / success than enquire whose soul dangles from his / watch-chain which would be embarrassing for both." People are greedy, self-serving, proud, and Cummings hates it. He adds a little self-deprecating sugar in the final lines to make this bitter pill of a poem go down a little smoother ("Humanity . . . you are / forever making poems in the lap / death Humanity // i hate you"), but it's not very subtle.

But his best work shows gift for associations, pitch-perfect diction, and masterful syntax. Cummings was, in many ways, more of a Romantic or a Georgian than a modernist, and behind the surface play of much of his work is a folk wisdom and wit. A poem like "[upon the room's]," which begins "upon the room's / silence,i will sew // a nagging button of candlelight / halfstooping to exactly kiss the trite // worm of her nakedness / until it go," possesses both a surgical exactitude and whimsy, a smoothness and a sonorous jaggedness, reflecting the conflicting impulses of love and lust, empathy and objectification, and oscillating moments of clarity and delusion. Poems like these increase after *50 Poems*, Cummings's seventh volume of poems, published in 1940 when he was forty-six. He never outgrows the burlesque, but meditative sonnets on love and spring—not as a metaphor for sex but as a personification of some benevolent, long-suffering life-giving being—increase. In *Tulips & Chimneys* (1922), spring is the "green" devil or a "speechless carnival" that ends in the "sweet / annihilation of swift / flesh." But in *Xaipe* (1950) it is "a mender of things":

> with eager
> fingers(with
> patient
> eyes)re
>
> -new-
>
> ing remaking what
> other
> -wise we should
> have thrown a-
>
> way(and whose
>
> brook
> -bright flower-
> soft bird
> -quick voice loves
>
> children
> and sunlight and
>
> mountains)in april(but
> if he should
> Smile)comes
>
> nobody'll know

A sonnet from *95 Poems* (1958) begins: "being to timelessness as it's to time, / love did no more begin than love will end; / where nothing is to breathe to stroll to swim / love is the air the ocean and the land."

In one of his final poems, Cummings writes: "o purple finch / please tell me why / this summer world (and you and i / who love some to live) / must die." The finch answers: "'if I / should tell you anything' / (that eagerly sweet caroling / self answers me) / 'I could not sing.'" This is Cummings at his best, and it is for poems like these that he will always be read.

11

Gertrud Kolmar's Silent Speech

THE FINAL LINE OF Gertrud Kolmar's early poem "Woman Undiscovered," written sometime before 1933, ends with eerie prescience. "I am a continent," she writes, "that one day soon will sink without a sound into the sea." The continent is the speaker's body that "no adventurer has claimed," whose "secrets" will die with it. But it's hard to read these lines without thinking of Kolmar's own hardly noticed disappearance in Nazi Germany in 1943, along with millions of other Jews.

Poet and critic Jacob Picard has called Kolmar "the greatest lyrical poetess of Jewish descent who has ever lived," but her work, if hardly unknown, has been obscured by the great tragedies of the war. And until recently, very little was known about her life. This has been rectified in part in Dieter Kühn's ambitious biography, translated into English by Linda Marianiello, which explores the poet's life and exhibits the best of her work—poems that alternately whisper like Sappho and rage like Medea.

Born in Berlin on December 4, 1894, Kolmar had an early life that seems idyllic. Her father, Ludwig Chodziesner (Kolmar was a pen name), was a renowned defense lawyer who counted many members of the aristocracy among his clients. Shy and readerly, with a soft spot for Robespierre and Napoleon, Kolmar studied at the upper girl's school in Charlottenburg before entering at seventeen the Arvedshof Country Women's School in Saxony—a home economics and agricultural school. This was an odd choice for the eldest daughter of a famous lawyer. Kolmar may have been considering a move to Palestine (she would live there, briefly, in 1939), which urgently needed farmers. But it is more likely that she studied at the school because of her keen and abiding interest in nature.

The defining moment of her early life came sometime before 1917 (the precise order of events is unclear) when she met a German officer named Karl Jodel. The two were most likely engaged to be married, but Kolmar became pregnant, and, according to Kühn, Jodel was assigned to the front. Whatever arrangement had been made was broken, and Kolmar had an abortion. At some point during this time she was sent to a sanatorium.

In 1923, the family left Berlin for a house with a garden in Neu-Finkenkrug, "a posh residential section west of Spandau." Kolmar worked as a tutor and a nanny in the first years following the move. She traveled to France sometime late in the summer of 1927 and returned home in October with a certificate in French language from the University of Dijon. From 1928 she cared full-time for her ailing mother, who died in 1930, and afterward worked and cared for her sixty-nine-year-old father until they were forced to move back to Berlin in 1939.

Kolmar published only seven poems between 1917 and 1934, but she continued to write poetry through these years. Many of her poems deal with motherhood and her overwhelming regret at the loss of the child. In "A Mother," for example, she addresses her "dearest one": "My child. / I touch you and with my mouth and nostrils / Like a lovely fruit inside a bowl / Where sweet and bitter mingle naturally." "Can you be," she asks, "anything I say?" In "Murder," the poet is "shackled" to her bed "with grating chains all gnawed with rust" and screams "Mother!" as she sees her dead child, "of dark green bronze, so stern and grave."

Kolmar is equally frank in her poems to an absent lover, which oscillate between tenderness and violent passion. In "Sea-Monster," for example, her lover has risen from the sea, his body "dripping cool and icy smooth." His arms embrace and soothe her. "And all my sheets," she writes, "smelled of the sea." In "Metamorphoses," however, the poet is a bat, hanging "rigid from a rafter." "Oh, man," she writes, "I dream your blood; my bite is death. / I'll claw into your hair and suck your breath."

Kolmar's nature poems on animal life and flowers are both whimsical and concrete. Toads are "low, fat, and wise," and a sunset cracks "the crystal laws," releasing a torrent of "flames" like "a golden net / Over a cherry tree in April." But it is in her final volume, *Worlds* (1937), that her originality and range are expressed most powerfully. In this cycle exploring places from the biblical world and from her own (Babel, Nineveh, the Urals, among others),

Kolmar becomes a visionary who sees a primordial womb that will continue to nourish life even at times of want or violence and offers, perhaps, a promise of future flourishing.

In "Out of Darkness," for example, a woman steps out into the night carrying a child—having "forgotten whose it is"—and walks towards the mountains. She passes a village whose streets are full of "Emaciated, greedy dogs," rotten fruit, and an "old man dress in rags." A door flies open and spits "ugly screams, demented, / howling, beastly cries" into the street. The old beggar, however, notices nothing but his "hunger and thirst." The woman comes to a "palace of the mighty," but it is empty except for a single room, illuminated by a single "midnight candle" and occupied by a "thinker" who tries to "invent" redemption "from his doubt." Below his window, two "horrid skeletons" argue over gold. The woman walks out of the town to a "stony, stubborn path," which leads to the mountains. When she arrives at its base, she climbs it with "groping hands" until she arrives at a cave. She enters and finds a huge "bronze-green, / nameless raven," crouches beneath the "sheltering shadows" and its "giant wings," and falls asleep listening to the "silent, growing word of my child" who "speaks . . . 'Til dawn."

What word the child speaks, Kolmar does not say, but like many of the poems in *Worlds*, the poet traces a decaying, decadent civilization that has become nearly lifeless while, at the same time, alluding to some possible rebirth or redemption, however faint. The resonance of the imagery of "Out of Darkness" with that of the Psalms—Kolmar's use of light and darkness, a pathway, a mountain refuge, and, most strikingly, the image of the woman hiding under the wing of a giant bird, which is evocative of Psalm 17, a psalm of David, where the speaker hides under the "shadow of the wing" of God—is unmistakable. In Psalm 17, David calls on God to protect him from "the wicked who do me violence" and who are like a lion, "eager to tear." He also asks God to fill the "womb" of his people "with treasure" and ends the psalm confidently stating that "I shall behold your face in righteousness; when I awake, I shall be satisfied with your likeness." There is no such confidence in Kolmar's poem. Yet, a hope remains. After all, the woman sleeps with her "brow turned eastward," which is, towards dawn.

Why did Kolmar remain in Germany while her brother, sister, and other family members left? Kolmar's sister, Hilde, had moved to Switzerland in 1938, and her brother had been sent to Australia in 1940, following a period in England? Her sister and her cousin, the philosopher Walter

Benjamin, had urged her to leave the country, but she remained with her father, who could not abandon the country that had abandoned him.

Similarly, in "Towers," the speaker of the poem walks on the coast of the sea and comes across an empty tower. Unlike the "palace of the mighty" in "Out of Darkness," the tower is completely empty, "Hard, dark, heavy, mute, in grayish desolation." It has no door or gate, and the only light it has is the "dim red glimmering / light" it reflects from its dark windows. Yet, all hope is not gone. "Somewhere," she writes, "far out, a ship wails in the ice." A "raven croaks his rasping prophecies." "Somewhere amid the forests of Bohemia," a birch tree dies. Yet, "bluebells dance around its feet." While the tower "stands alone," its only life that of a female scorpion who "gives birth to living / young, and dies," at night, from its "deepest being" rises a "shy and gentle, quickly dying tone / Of a long forgotten harp."

There is no doubt that caring for her father was an important part of Kolmar's own decision to stay. Kühn also suggests that it may have been that leaving Germany for Kolmar would have been to leave the very soil of her imagination—an imagination that was, in effect, her life. Kolmar suggested as much herself. In one of her later poems, "Asia," she wrote: "Yours is the vision, . . . You live to be, if not to act." Kolmar's father was deported to Theresienstadt in September 1942. Four months later, Kolmar was sent to Auschwitz. She was forty-eight—her voice, which we find in her poems, a "long forgotten harp," if rarely shy or gentle.

12

What Happened to Basil Bunting?

BASIL BUNTING'S LONG POEM "Briggflatts" is one of the masterpieces of the twentieth century. Written in 1965, when the British poet was sixty-five and working as a lowly subeditor for the Newcastle *Daily Journal*, it traces Bunting's life from his days in a Northumbrian Quaker school, early imprisonment, and time in Italy to his service as a spy and officer in World War II and his return home to oblivion.

Like other great modernist works, it is fragmented and abstract, yet richly textured and sonorous. Its topic is unfulfilled love and failed ambition. While the poet starts out in life bragging like a "sweet tenor bull" dancing "tiptoe," before long he is "mating / beauty with squalor to beget lines still born." Cyril Connolly called "Briggflatts" the "finest long poem . . . since T. S. Eliot's *Quartets*," and Thom Gunn remarked that it was "one of the few great poems of this century." But it and the poet are now mostly forgotten. Bunting knew Eliot, and W. B. Yeats. He was a close friend of Ezra Pound's, and he corresponded regularly with William Carlos Williams and Louis Zukofsky. Yet he published too little in those days of "high modernism" to establish a lasting reputation.

The Beats—whom Bunting thought were very friendly people but very poor poets—helped bring him the attention he deserved in the 1960s and '70s, but interest began to fade in the 1980s. In 1988, just three years after his death, Hugh Kenner complained that most people were unfamiliar with Bunting's work. His poems went out of print and have remained so until recently.

What Happened to Basil Bunting?

Richard Burton's exhaustive if verbose biography of Bunting, *A Strong Song Tows Us*, goes a long way to restoring Bunting to his rightful place among the greats of Anglo-American literary modernism. Born to a medical doctor in an upper-middle-class family in Northumbria, Bunting was educated at Quaker schools—the only child in the family to receive such an education. His parents were not religious, but they may have sent Bunting to the Quakers because of his sensitivity, depression, and occasional paranoia. As a child and as a man, Bunting could be implacable, self-absorbed, and insolent, but also of strong principle. During the First World War, Bunting was a conscientious objector. He was one of roughly 16,500 men who refused to fight—but one of only a little over a thousand who refused even nonmilitary service. He was sent to prison, where he did not do any work that contributed to the war effort and went on a hunger strike when he was not let out following the armistice. Following his eventual release from prison, Bunting studied for a couple of years at the London School of Economics. While he had a mind for numbers and economic theory, his true passion was poetry. In 1923, he left for Paris, with no money and no job, to visit Ezra Pound, whom he had met in London. Pound introduced him to Ford Madox Ford, who employed Bunting for a time to work on his newly founded *Transatlantic Review*. Bunting returned to England after his father died and moved in 1925 to London, where he worked for the next three years for the conservative *Outlook* as a financial journalist.

Bunting's politics are a little difficult to pin down. He expressed some sympathy for communism when he was younger, and he was a member of the Fabian Society until 1923. Zukofsky called him "a British-conservative-antifascist-imperialist." In reality, he was more of a classical liberal, albeit with a hefty skepticism of laissez-faire capitalism—a staunch individualist with a deep dislike and distrust of all forms of authority.

In 1947, Bunting wrote Pound's wife: "I am for thwarting the government—all governments, especially the more powerful and effective ones; and for not reforming backwards nations; and for pushing economics out of the limelight for a century or so; and limiting free compulsory education to reading, writing and 'rithmatic." Alluding to Allen Ginsberg in a letter to Jonathan Williams in 1973, Bunting wrote: "I detest Gurus, Tibetan or any other breed."

During his three years in London, Bunting wrote his first notable poem, "Villon," which is loosely based on his various imprisonments (in England and later, for lack of proper paperwork, in Norway and Russia).

It is named after a medieval French poet much lauded by Pound: François Villon, whose occasionally bawdy *Testament*, written during his imprisonment in a Paris jail, skewered local clergy and magistrates. Bunting's "Villon" is more philosophical but equally biting and blunt.

In 1928, Bunting left London to join Pound in Rapallo. Two years later, he married an American woman, Marian Culver, with whom he would have three children. The couple lived in Italy, Spain, and England before they divorced in 1939. The poet never met his third child and only son, Rustam, who was born after Marian and Bunting separated in 1937 and who died of polio while away at school in 1952. When England entered World War II, Bunting, who had been wandering around the United States looking for work, returned home immediately to enlist.

Why this sudden change in principle? "During the First World War," Bunting remarked afterwards, "it was possible to believe, I did believe, that it was a totally unnecessary war fought for purely selfish ends, to get hold of markets and things like that. You couldn't believe that in the second one at all. It was perfectly obvious for years beforehand that nothing short of war and violence would ever stop Hitler and his appalling career." While he at first had difficulty enlisting and obtaining a post, he was eventually accepted by the RAF and sent to Persia as a translator. Bunting had for years been translating the work of the tenth-century Persian poet Hakim Abdu'l Qasim Ferdowsi. He initially struggled as a war translator since he had never heard modern Persian spoken until he arrived in Ahwaz, near the Iranian border. One of the first things Bunting was called on to translate was a court martial. "I hope they put the right man in jail," he later quipped. But Bunting would rise quickly. He moved from translation to espionage to first officer and later Vice-Consul in Isfahan, where he was in charge of all intelligence in the region. He was extremely knowledgeable of the region's customs and politics and knew many of the local chiefs.

Bunting loved Persia. It was, he wrote, "one of the most civilized countries in the world." While Europe was ravaged, Bunting lived a relatively comfortable life. "I am sure you would like Isfahan," he wrote Karl Drerup, "My lawn is studded with bright flowers, just like a Persian brocade. . . . I have a nice Persian house built around a garden, and another garden opening from it, where there are fruit trees, and where I keep my five alarming watch-dogs. Beyond, there is a brook, and then more gardens."

He liked, he wrote Dorothy Pound, the "more physical, less logical" life in Persia, and it is no surprise that, reflecting on the war in 1971, Bunting told an interviewer, "I can say with complete immorality that I enjoyed the war very much." Bunting's self-absorption was one of the reasons for the failure of his first marriage, and it would rear its ugly head from time to time throughout his life. But he was almost always honest—with himself and with others, whatever the price to him or them.

After the war, Bunting returned to Persia to work for the British Foreign Office, but he was forced to resign when he married a local woman, Sima Alladadian. He found a job as a correspondent for *The Times*, reporting on the increasingly unstable political situation in the region. Eventually, Bunting, who remained longer than any other British reporter, had to evacuate in 1952. He was seen by locals as supporting British interests in the region, and he was under regular threat of assassination and became the object of at least two attempts.

The Times left Bunting out to dry—or at least, Bunting believed so. When he returned to Britain, the paper did not assign another position to him, and he found regular employment elusive, for various reasons, until he settled for the editing position at the small *Daily Journal*, which he loathed. He more or less disappeared from the public eye until twelve years later, when Tom Pickard appeared at his door and drew Bunting back into circulation and, unbeknownst to Pickard, sparked Bunting's composition of "Briggflatts."

For all the poem's formal inventiveness, Bunting's carefully crafted, tightly packed lines ring with significance. In "Briggflatts," images of stone and water, voices on the air, sea, and grass, reoccur to capture the fleeting beauty of love, the shortness of life, and the folly of ambition. The lesson of his work, and experience, is that human knowledge is absurdly limited, that love is magical but short-lived. While the poem begins with the image of a young bull, dancing in the fields in May, in the background, we hear the sound of a mason's mallet, striking rock to the beat of the "lark's twitter." What is he making? A gravestone. The "stone spells a name," but names "none"—that is, one who is no longer. Ironically, the lark's song coupled with the sound the mallet reminds us that we all will "rot." The image of the gravestone reappears throughout the rest of the poem. Unlike the songs of birds, the stone remains, reminding us of death's permanence in the face of life's transience. Death also outlasts love, and perhaps music and poetry.

The sea also swallows all—ships, sailors, goods—and the songs of those who sing while riding on it, Bunting writes. Yet, the sea is sensuous. Fish "sing" as they break the surface. A taste of "garlic and salt" hover above it. Its foam is a "white wine," and its breeze makes olives and "hillside / blue figs" speak. All of this makes poetry seem "a pedant's game." In many ways, the poem is about the superiority of nature's verse compared to man's, as it speaks with beautiful honesty about life and death. And yet, Bunting shows this possible superiority in a poem. For Rilke, the poet draws this beauty out of nature—gives it a fullness of being—through poetry. For Stevens, the poet superimposes this tragic beauty on nature. For Bunting, it seems, poetry is simply the act of repeating the music we hear in the world—a music that is, by turns, dark and light. The poet himself is part of nature and, therefore, unable to place himself outside it—a position that is assumed in both Rilke and Stevens's theory of poetry to some degree. As Bunting put it in the "Coda" to the poem, a "strong song" pulls us out to sea, like a current pulls a boat, and we follow it to another country "we do not know."

13

Elizabeth Bishop's Artistry

IN A MOSTLY LAUDATORY review of her *Collected Poems* in 1969, John Ashbery wrote that Elizabeth Bishop was "somehow an establishment poet," which is to say that she wasn't exactly, probably because the word "establishment" was as meaningless in 1969 as it is today.

For poets and critics who like to keep such lists, Bishop has always been a problem. She was a lesbian who held onto her Baptist propriety throughout life. ("I don't like words like 'loins', 'groins', 'crotch', 'flanks', 'thighs,'" she once wrote to the poet May Swenson. "They are in general ugly words that startle the reader.") She had little interest in creating a "new" poetry that replicated the techniques of the other arts or supposedly broke free of all moral or aesthetic constraints. She was shy and, unlike Charles Olson or Allen Ginsberg, uninterested in bombast or self-promotion. She spent many of her adult years not in New York or London or Paris, but in Key West (six years) and Brazil (fourteen). She won the Pulitzer Prize in 1956, but wrote little, completing only five slim books of poetry and publishing just 101 poems, including translations, in over fifty years of writing. While she taught at Harvard toward the end of her life, some of her courses attracted as few as five students (one of whom was Dana Gioia).

For many critics, one of the defining characteristics of Bishop's work is her constraint. So it is, too, for Irish novelist Colm Tóibín, who argues in *On Elizabeth Bishop* that unlike the confessional poems of Robert Lowell, a long-time friend and regular correspondent, Bishop's work was rooted in personal experience but devoid of overly personal details and melodrama. Poetry, for her, "was not self-expression" he writes, but a form of truth-telling in which "there is very little that can be said, but there is much that can be suggested."

Tóibín regularly remarks on "what is left out" of the poems. Her early poem "Roosters," for example, was written shortly after the Navy arrived in Key West, "much to Bishop's annoyance." It describes the noisy and violent lives of roosters (and hens) with her trademark casual precision, but it also could be read, Tóibín writes, as an "antiwar poem" or a condemnation of "a world run by men." Yet, it shouldn't—or it shouldn't *only* be read as these things. It is also a poem about morning, Tóibín argues, and, of course, about roosters. To reduce it to the immediate contexts of its composition is to miss its "immense suggestive power."

"The Armadillo," another of Bishop's relatively early works, is "infused ... with a sense of loss," Tóibín writes, while the voice of the poem somehow "remains at the edge of things." In a late poem on a painting by her great-uncle in which she recognizes the landscape of her early childhood in Nova Scotia, the tone is one of "helpless reverie, infinite and puzzled regret" but with "no direct mention ... of how she might feel."

In her most widely read poem, "One Art," which begins, "The art of losing isn't hard to master," and lists the many things in life the speaker has lost ("door keys," "my mother's watch," "two cities"), including a "you" in the final stanza, Tóibín writes that what Bishop doesn't mention is losing her father (who died before she turned one), her mother (who was institutionalized when she was five), and her partner, Lota de Macedo Soares (who committed suicide in 1967). To have mentioned these, Tóibín thinks, may have ruined the tension between stoicism and self-pity.

Bishop's artistry is in using concrete actions and objects to evoke particular emotions without stating them directly. Like Emily Dickinson, Bishop understood that poetry tells truth's "slant," or, in Tóibín's words, somehow communicates the "unmentionable." That the arts, including poetry, communicate indirectly is hardly a new idea, but in an age of increasingly political or (merely) personal poems, it may be worth remembering.

Bishop's many startling similes and metaphors are, in my view, among the greatest pleasures of reading her. Bishop's work is full of them. Peninsulas "take the water between thumb and finger / like women feeling for the smoothness of yard-goods." An iceberg, "[l]ike jewelry from the grave ... saves itself perpetually and adorns / only itself." A storm roams the sky "uneasily / like a dog looking for a place to sleep." A beach "hisses like fat."

Take Bishop's long poem, "The Moose," for example. At first it seems to have no recognizable theme. The first four stanzas describe the "narrow provinces" of Bishop's Nova Scotia. These stanzas are part of a single sentence and are actually a parenthesis of sorts. If this parenthesis were removed the poem would read: "From narrow province / of fish and bread and tea . . . a bus journeys west."

The second section of the poem deals with the people on the bus and the conversations the speaker of the poem overhears. Bishop uses repetition, both to create a fugue-like crescendo and to highlight the redundancy of the landscape that is also a dreamlike "divagation," a "slow hallucination." The final section of the poem begins when a moose steps in front of the bus. The repetition stops after this, and while subtle, marks a break in the seemingly dreamlike voyage, where things are seen over and over again and come in and out of focus.

What does the moose stand for? At first, it seems to stand for art itself, a break from the redundant landscape that lulls the passengers on the bus to sleep. The responses on the bus seem to support this. The moose is "otherworldly" and "curious" who creates a "sweet / sensation of joy." At the same time, she is "awful plain" and has woken the passengers from their sleep. In this case, she is not a symbol of art but of reality. Which is it? For Bishop, both.

14

Yves Bonnefoy's Pursuit of Presence

"If I had to sum up in a sentence the impression Shakespeare makes upon me," the poet Yves Bonnefoy wrote in an early essay, "I should say that, in his work, I see no opposition between the universal and the particular."

This is exactly the opposition that Bonnefoy—one of France's greatest contemporary poets, who was regularly named as a possible Nobel laureate until his death in 2016—wished to eliminate in his own work. From his first major book of poems, *On the Motion and Immobility of Douve* (1953), to a recent selection of poetry and prose, *Second Simplicity* (2012), Bonnefoy devoted himself to what he calls in his poetry the universal "here" and the eternal "now," to the impossible but hopeful pursuit of "presence." In "A Bit of Water" (1991), he writes:

> I long to grant eternity
> To this flake
> That alights on my hand,
> By making my life, my warmth,
> My past, my present days
> Into a moment: the boundless
> Moment of now
>
> But already it's no more
> Than a bit of water, lost in the fog
> Of bodies moving through snow.

Yves Bonnefoy's Pursuit of Presence

Born in Tours in 1923 to a railway worker and a teacher, Bonnefoy studied mathematics, philosophy, and the history of science before turning to full-time teaching, writing, and translation (notably of Shakespeare). His early work was heavily influenced by surrealism. He found surrealist imagery, such as Max Ernst's collages and an Alberto Giacometti sculpture of a peach-like sphere dangling above an abstract wedge (1930–31), to be both profoundly present—"simple," as he puts it—and deeply ambiguous. For Bonnefoy, it is ambiguity that provides the poetic image with its vibrancy, the image's combination of the abstract and the concrete making it "deeply akin . . . to a temple, to the dwelling of a god."

In *Anti-Plato*, a long poem published in 1947, the temple is a rather gory one: "The country of blood, spreads its dark currents under the dress / When one says, Here the flesh of night begins and the false paths choke with sand." But in *On the Motion and Immobility of Douve* (Douve is a mythical feminine figure of Bonnefoy's creation), violence and death are transformed into images of a subtle and strange beauty. "I see Douve," Bonnefoy writes, "stretched out. In the scarlet city of air, where / branches clash across her face, where roots find their way into her / body—she radiates a strident insect joy, a frightful music."

Like René Magritte, Bonnefoy would come to see a connection between Catholicism's sacred mysteries and surrealism's worship of the "marvelous" image. In a 1959 lecture, Bonnefoy suggested that the goal of poetry is to renew the material world through language, just as Christ, the Word, redeemed the material world by taking on flesh. The difficulty facing the poet is that human words detach themselves from the objects they are supposed to evoke, presenting themselves as direct, autonomous expressions of a purely spiritual knowledge. Thus modern poetry, according to Bonnefoy, has tended toward a sort of falsehood, repeatedly denying the very world it should renew.

Bonnefoy identified Eliot's *The Waste Land* as the first work to recognize the dead modern spiritual landscape—"that desolate land, where a spell has dried up the springs"—that comes from this rejection of the spiritual element of the material world. This does not mean that the poet, like Eliot, should return to Christianity. ("Christianity," Bonnefoy writes, "only affirms the individual existence for a brief instant. The created thing is brought back to God by means of Providence and thus deprived once again of its absolute value.") Nor should the poet give up on the spiritual landscape. Instead, he should return to the difficult and perhaps never-ending task of naming the concrete world to remedy spiritual exhaustion. "Yet, let us not abandon this blank and empty horizon," he admonishes; "let us hold our ground, *le pas gagné* [the step gained]."

Land or "ground" is an apt metaphor for Bonnefoy's *oeuvre*. All of his poems are inextricably linked to the places where they were written. For much of his adult life, Bonnefoy spent his summers with his wife in an abandoned monastery in Provence. "There was," Bonnefoy believes, "more of the real here than anywhere else." There he wrote many of the poems that make up *Written Stone* (1965) and *In the Lure of the Threshold* (1975). They express both a deep sense of separation from the world and an unexpected connection to it. Life is one of "Unscalable solitude, and so many paths!" Yet the world is also miraculously present, as he writes in "A Stone" (1965):

> We walked past those meadows
> Where a whole god sometimes dropped from a tree
> (And it was a token for us, toward evening).
>
> I pushed you silently,
> I felt your weight against our pensive hands,
> O you, my dark words,
> Gates across the roads of evening.

In such moments of communion, Bonnefoy writes, "time stays around us like pools of color." It is his hope that these "dark words" of poetry will somehow rescue Eliot's "desolate land," even if only partially, from the oblivion of lifelessness. "Have faith, redeemed earth," he writes. "A sense may grow in your words, as transparency / Grows in the grapes of aging summer."

In the 1980s, Bonnefoy's poetry developed narrative qualities and a simplified diction—perhaps influenced by his trading in Provence for New England and other places and acquiring with them a new language of daily intercourse. The poems of *Beginning and End of the Snow* (1991) have an easy whimsicality while maintaining their seriousness. In "The Garden," he writes:

> It's snowing.
> Under the flakes, a door opens at last
> On the garden beyond the world.
>
> I set out. But my scarf

> Snags on a rusty nail,
> And the cloth of my dreams is torn.

There is nothing to do but keep moving (and writing): "I move forward," Bonnefoy writes in "The Only Rose" (1991). "The purest form is still the shape / That mist inhabits, and dissolves. / Trampled snow is the only rose."

This push toward greater simplicity in his own verse grew as Bonnefoy continued translating Shakespeare. 1957 TO HIS DEATH, he translated more than a dozen plays and a selection of the sonnets. As he notes in a preface to his edition of "Hamlet," the goal is not simply to "transpose" English into French but to translate the "allegorical" sense of the play by rendering Shakespeare's characters both immediate and concrete. Verbosity, Bonnefoy suggests, tends to dilute the reality and, therefore, the significance of the characters. This effort to capture the reality of Shakespeare's characters with simple, direct concision no doubt refined Bonnefoy's effort to do the same with elements of his own experience.

Second Simplicity includes a number of short prose pieces, some of which have never been translated into English. Some are serious. In "Three Recollections of Borges," for example, Bonnefoy recalls three meetings with Jorge Luis Borges, ending with a visit in Geneva just before Borges's death. As Bonnefoy left, Borges's voice echoed down the hospital hall, urging him to be mindful of "Virgil *and* Verlaine." Other pieces are wonderfully farcical, imagining, for example, a production of "Hamlet" in the Alps. Most of the actors' time is spent climbing, with Ophelia ironically leading the way.

Poetry, Bonnefoy suggested in 1959, is "hope," and as *Second Simplicity* shows, he lost little faith or vigor in his final years. Yet, even as he continued to search for that enduring presence here on earth, the idea that such a presence may also be elsewhere, perhaps even more fully so, is no longer dismissed outright but wistfully entertained, as in "Passer-by, These Are Words" (2001):

> And for you who now move on, pensively,
> Here becomes there without ceasing to be.

15

André du Bouchet's Fragments

ALL LITERARY WORKS ARE fragments of a kind. However complex the plot, deep the characters, nuanced the feelings, or multifarious the images, possibilities remain unmentioned, details uninvented, feelings muted, and angles unexplored. The satisfaction that even great novels or poems provide is a momentary fullness. There is always more to be said or felt, and it is in this sense that no work is ever complete.

But not all works are *fragmentary*. Some—mostly from the twentieth and twenty-first centuries—are full of gaps, disconnected phrases, clashing images, and shifts in situation and tone. Others are not. The connection between images and events is clear. We may think of the former as "postmodern" *texts*—poems or novels that undermine coherence as an attack on meaning—but this lumps very different works into a single, rather useless category. Not all fragmentation means the same thing. Sometimes it is used to say less, but sometimes more.

One poet who uses fragmentation to say more is André du Bouchet (1924–2001), an under-recognized poet's poet in his native France who is almost entirely unknown in English despite living and studying in America for eight years. In *Openwork*, a selection of du Bouchet's poetry and notebooks from across his career published in Yale's wonderful Margellos series, du Bouchet is preoccupied with reality. For him, we see but don't see the world and ourselves. "The profound coherence," he writes, "of certain superficial, ill-assorted images" can blind us to the particularities of a tree, stone, or blade of grass. The task of the poet is to bring us face-to-face, however momentarily, with these objects by "flay[ing] the senses." This is not an attack on the order of things but an attempt to see through it to creation's complexity. When a poem is "too clear," du Bouchet writes, "you see nothing."

Born in Paris in 1924 to a medical doctor of Russian-Jewish descent and a schizophrenic father who was trained—but rarely worked—as an engineer, du Bouchet grew up in the city's well-to-do Sixteenth Arrondissement. In 1940, the du Bouchets fled German-occupied France on the last passenger ship out of Lisbon to Boston. Du Bouchet's paternal grandfather, who was a successful physician in Paris but who was born in Philadelphia, had returned to the United States a year earlier and helped the family initially, but he could not support them indefinitely. Du Bouchet's mother restarted her medical studies since her diploma was not recognized in America. His father was institutionalized, and du Bouchet and his younger sister, Hélène, were sent to boarding school. Du Bouchet then attended Amherst College, from which he graduated *summa cum laude*, before earning an MA in English at Harvard and returning to his native France in 1948.

As Hoyt Rogers points out in his introduction to *Openwork*, du Bouchet's eight-year "sojourn," as he called it, was unwanted but instrumental to his development as a poet. Du Bouchet wrote his mother in 1947 that his time in America was "neither lovely nor dreadful. It has simply been a necessity, ... a condition of my life," but, as Rogers notes, it allowed him to master English and separated him from his own language, which helped to highlight the connection between feelings and words—one of du Bouchet's preoccupations. Rogers notes that in a conversation with du Bouchet less than a year before he died, the poet "recalled that in this period English was the language in which he 'didn't sputter,' whereas French was the language of intimacy, 'of everything that belonged to the order of muteness.' After his long exile in America, he noted, French seemed 'like a foreign language.'"

On his return to France, du Bouchet married Tina Jolas and, with the help of research grants and fellowships, which he did not always use for their intended purposes, began writing and studying poetry. He became a student of René Char (who would later have an affair with du Bouchet's wife) and the work of Pierre Reverdy and Francis Ponge. He became good friends with Yves Bonnefoy (with whom he founded the short-lived but influential journal *L'Éphémère*), as well as with many of the major writers and artists of his day, including Paul Celan, Philippe Jaccottet, and Alberto Giacometti. Yet, he eschewed the surrealism that was still popular in France in the 1950s and was skeptical of intellectual and literary trends. Instead of Paris, he preferred the French countryside—first in Normandy, then around the village of Truinas in southeastern France, where he bought a house in 1971. Du Bouchet would often take notes and write lines into a notebook while on long walks. Some of these he would revise and publish in small presses. Others he left unchanged.

In his earlier work and notebooks, du Bouchet is at his most prosaic. He turns frequently to the nature of writing: clarity, he believes, can be calming but deadly. It's comforting to read "stories of fire" in "Black letters big as birds," he writes. We "fear we've lost what we love," and "Our remorse feeds on scenes that we rehearse":

> Pleasures filtered by night turn to brine,
> like a feeling we experience upside-down:
> a mirror-image, such is the placid hell of trees
> in the gleaming brook. Their branches smile,
> dangle free

Here du Bouchet, who received a Greek scholarship to Amherst, is most likely responding to Aristotle's idea that the value of tragedy is found in its "catharsis"—its ability to "purge" or "cleanse" our excessive passions, in particular, fear and pity. But for du Bouchet, mimesis (the "mirror-image") does not liberate us from the "fear we've lost what we love." It keeps it alive, transforming it into a "placid hell . . . in the gleaming brook." "I refuse this tender alphabet," he writes. "Burn, Burn, and always Burn / and forever the frenzy of chains / and pointless thirst and ravenous fire." Better knowledge of life's "pointless thirst" than the delusion of freedom.

Du Bouchet's critique of mimesis is not an attack on poetry's obligation to reflect reality. Rather, mimesis is vulnerable to oversimplifications. Instead of letters "big as birds," du Bouchet turns to blank spaces; and instead of shaping his words "around the hero," he uses "words made of much silence." The ready-made stories we tell ourselves, "the images rolling under [our] brow," have clouded our vision. "What's left of the man himself so thoroughly trampled and smudged out," du Bouchet asks rhetorically, "whose outline on the sidewalk is so sharp?" This brings us back to du Bouchet's preoccupation with the object. For du Bouchet, to look out on the world, to see it in its particularities, is also to see ourselves more clearly. "Man," du Bouchet writes, "is the conscious part of reality; man is reality's head."

André du Bouchet's Fragments

There is an element of Eastern mysticism here. Rogers argues that "there is no such thing as 'mysticism' in du Bouchet's work, much less a personification of the sacred," though he admits "there is undeniably a profound strain of self-abnegation." "All he professes," Rogers continues, "is that beyond our limits there is otherness." But du Bouchet says more than this. The earth is "immense," full of a life that it cannot easily contain. The sky "heaves . . . above the earth," and the sun is an "unharnessed fire," an "unconsumed fire igniting us like a / tree along the slope." In fact, the poet is frequently overwhelmed by the earth's grandeur:

> I am in the field
> like a drop of water
> on a red-hot iron
> the field
> eclipses itself
> the stones open
> like a stack of plates
> held
> in the arms
> when evening breathes
> I stay
> with these cold white plates
> as if I held the earth
> itself
> in my arms

Du Bouchet can't avoid using personification. The earth speaks. He writes of his "relationship" to reality. Here he holds the field like a child—a field that is alive but also enlivened by something greater than both itself and the poet.

At the same time, the earth "strips us bare." It remains, but we "dissipate." "Alone I inhabit this white / place," du Bouchet writes, "where nothing thwarts the wind." For du Bouchet, the task of the poet is to face the earth's grandeur and cruel impersonality with courage and without delusion. This means longing for continuity, for something beyond the "silent . . . wall": feeling deeply without ever finding satisfaction. Yet, even du Bouchet cannot prevent his sort of perpetual openness from sounding dogmatic and his belief in the absence of satisfaction from smacking, well, of satisfaction. "I found myself / free / and without hope," he writes at one point, which we are meant to find laudatory (so much for self-abnegation), and intones: "Nothing satisfies me. I satisfy nothing."

The translations themselves are marvelous. Paul Auster revised his translations of du Bouchet's *In the Vacant Heat* and *Where the Sun*, and Rogers, who has translated the poetry of Yves Bonnefoy and the fiction of Philippe Claudel, took care of the earlier and later work. Here we have a poet whose lines often contain worlds—a master of the image, who possesses an exactitude that makes his poems, whatever his attitude towards desire and other faults, a pure pleasure to read.

16

Vernon Scannell's Wounded Music

IN 1949, VERNON SCANNELL (1922–2007) was working at an English fairground boxing booth, taking a fall in one fight and avenging himself on a hapless challenger in the next. Behind him were convictions for bigamy and desertion, an abusive childhood, short stints as a professional boxer and a private university tutor (despite never having gone to university himself), innumerable bar fights, and a single book of poems.

Ahead were more women, more bar fights, more time in prison, more teaching, and more poems. At the time, he was thirty-seven and living with his divorced mother, writing little. His life seemed to be at a dead end. But as James Andrew Taylor notes in this excellent biography of the poet, an opportunity arrived, as would happen many times in Scannell's life, to pull himself—or to be pulled—from the rubble. In this case, it was a job teaching English and history at a secondary school in West London. At other times, it was meeting a new woman, receiving a small prize or grant, or even having a chance encounter with some old friends.

The seeming incongruity of Vernon Scannell's life and personality makes him one of the most intriguing figures of contemporary literature. He was a man of immense sensitivity who identified with the weak, the broken, and the cowardly of the world but, when drunk, was a terrible wife beater. He loved children and despised violence but fought in the Second World War and had a lifelong passion for boxing. He was one of the most talented poets of his generation, but he often felt out of place in literary circles and regularly doubted his talent.

He was talented though, and mostly self-taught. Scannell's poems combine frank statement and penetrating insight in carefully crafted lines. In "Mastering the Craft," which compares his two great passions—boxing and poetry—Scannell wrote that poets, like boxers, "must train."

> Practise metre's footwork, learn
> The old iambic left and right,
> To change the pace and how to hold
> The big punch till the proper time,
> Jab away with accurate rhyme;
> Adapt the style or be knocked cold.

He was a blue-collar poet, though this does not do justice to the range of his work, which deals with love, war, sports, childhood, and, most of all, failure—often with self-effacing humor. When he was in jail in 1974 for drunk driving, his daughter Nancy wrote to ask him what a jailbird was. Scannell wrote:

> His plumage is dun,
> His appetite indiscriminate.
> He has no mate.
> His nest is built of brick and steel;
> He sings at night
> A long song, sad and silent.
> He cannot fly.

This is classic Scannell: honest, direct, almost entirely defeated except for the elegant formulation of that defeat. For Scannell, a poet must know his craft, but if he lacks passion, his poems are useless. In "The Poet's Tongue," he writes: "With industry and patience he must bring / Together his great arsenal." Yet the poet ultimately ignores his "intricate machines" to use "bits of flint that hit the target square."

Scannell was born John Vernon Bain in 1922. His father was a photographer, and Vernon, his older brother, and a younger sister grew up in the small town of Aylesbury, where a nearby RAF base provided a regular source of customers for photography services. Life was hard at home: Both Scannell and his brother suffered regular beatings from their father. This was not the sort of firm but corrective punishment common at the time, but violent whippings, burnings, and slaps to the face, all accompanied by derisive mocking.

As the boys grew, the slaps became punches. Their mother was unaffectionate and frequently blamed the boys for provoking their father. Scannell and his brother both developed an early love of reading—against all odds, it would seem—and found some solace in P. G. Wodehouse, *David Copperfield*, and Sir Walter Scott—although this had to be hidden from their father, who viewed reading as the mark of a sissy.

At twelve, Scannell took up boxing and discovered that he had a gift for it. He would go on to fight briefly as a professional and would use his skill, as we have seen, to earn some extra money here and there. Later, Scannell would remember his time in the ring fondly, describing an opponent's head "jerking back as if on an invisible puppet-wire" and "a grey tidal wave of noise" sweeping over him—"warm and exalting."

Scannell left school at fourteen to work as a bookkeeper for an insurance company. He was tall, handsome, and charming. At eighteen he met a young woman by the name of Barbara Phillips. She became pregnant, and Scannell quickly married her, but the two would never live together. Scannell and his brother stole close to £100 from their father and went on a weeklong drinking binge in London. Running short of cash, they enlisted in the army.

Scannell saw time in North Africa, though less than he suggested in his memoirs. He was not present at the Battle of El Alamein, but he almost certainly fought at the Battle of the Mareth Line and the assault on Wadi Akarit. He also took part in the D-Day invasion. Scannell was not the best soldier: He would regularly go AWOL during training to go on drinking binges, and on the battlefield, he tried as much as possible to avoid shooting anybody. After the attack on Wadi Akarit, however, he snapped when he saw British soldiers stealing from their own fallen comrades: "I just remember all those dead Seaforths lying out there," he later recalled, "and our blokes going round, settling on them like fucking flies, taking their watches and wallets and Christ-knows-what, and I just got up and walked. It was like a dream." He was arrested a few days later and spent six months in a military prison in Alexandria before being released for good behavior and reinstated with his unit.

Scannell's time in a military prison was not only difficult—the prisoners were given repetitive tasks, regularly humiliated, and subjected to random punishments—but it instilled in him a strong sense of guilt and self-doubt. Afterwards, he would always see himself as a coward, despite having deserted only after the fighting ended at Wadi Akarit and going on to fight in Normandy. James Andrew Taylor writes that Alexandria reinforced Scannell's "distrust of military virtues . . . and . . . brought to his poetry a sympathy of the weak, the morally compromised."

The day after Germany surrendered in 1945, Scannell (still Bain) packed his bags and left his post. Because this was considered a second desertion, Scannell, if caught, would be returned to military prison to finish his original sentence. In London, he fell in with a group of artists and intellectuals who had opposed the war from the beginning and who took Scannell in, providing him with a new name and work on the black market. In 1947, he was caught by military police, faced trial for desertion, and was sent to a psychiatric hospital for a short time before being released. He married again, though he had never divorced his first wife, and was subsequently charged with bigamy.

It was in London that Scannell began to write seriously. He would marry a third time, and remain married for two decades, before divorcing again. While he worked as a secondary school teacher and headmaster to support his growing family, he lived mostly by his writing and readings. According to Taylor, he was a good (if often absent) father and a loving and terrifying spouse who could become violent when drunk. He found it impossible to remain faithful to one woman.

Scannell was a prolific, as well as talented, writer: Between 1960 and 1990 he published more than a book a year. His two final collections contain some of his most powerful work as he looks back, with regret, on his life. In "Missing Things," for example, Scannell writes: "I'm very old and breathless, tired and lame, / And soon I'll be no more to anyone / Than the slowly fading trochee of my name." While the poet tells himself that, when dead, he will feel nothing, "like the stone of which the house is made," he asks: "Then why so sad? And just a bit afraid?" The reason, of course, is that just as there is more to life than poetry, there may be more to death than silence. In one poem, Scannell confesses his "need to give a full account of all / the lies and self cruelties; in another, he hears the first soft chords from far away: / the wounded music of what might have been."

Whether or not the poet found peace at the end of his life, his own "wounded music"—quiet, elegant, humble—rang true to the end.

17

Allen Ginsberg, Bore

IN THE FORWARD TO *Wait Till I'm Dead*—a selection of Allen Ginsberg's uncollected poems published in 2016—Rachel Zucker explains why we should read his poetry: He's "dangerous! So, come and get some!" And he never disappoints. "Years later," she writes, "after countless readings, his poems still feel *hot* to me." In slightly more adult language, he subverts traditional morals and is stunningly original.

She's right that almost all of Ginsberg's poems are about sex or spirituality, which are more or less the same for him ("the endless Being / one creature that gives birth to itself / thrills in its minutest particular"—to give one of the few quotable passages on the topic). When they aren't, they're about politics, except "Kaddish" (1960), which is about his mother and is probably his best poem.

But one thing Ginsberg isn't is original. Or, to put it more accurately, he is original but almost always in the same way. In his *Collected Poems*, Ginsberg occasionally shows an excellent ear and an eye for suffering or joy. Poems like "Who Be Kind To" (1965) is, at least initially, a wonderfully practical poem infused with sympathy. "Be kind to your neighbor who weeps / solid tears on the television sofa," he writes. Focusing on the smallest details instead of the striking ocean view, "Bixby Canyon Ocean Path Word Breeze" (1971) is an example of concision and evocative description. But his work as a whole is surprisingly predictable. "Howl" (1956), his most celebrated poem, may have been new in its assimilation of various influences and its use of smut. Following the surrealists, it combines religious language with vulgarity and uses clashing noun phrases instead of narrative, replacing end rhyme (which Ginsberg used regularly in his early work) with Walt Whitman's catalogs (the repetition of a single word to begin each line). After "Howl," however, these techniques overwhelm almost every poem. Once the drumbeat of noun phrases takes hold of Ginsberg's mind, there's nothing to do but wait until the fit passes.

"Wichita Vortex Sutra," for example, is one of his better efforts in his effusive, chanting, semi-disconnected, Whitmanesque style. Still the oscillation between an accumulation of clauses and catalogs can be tiresome. The repetition of sentence structures and certain key words with some variation in the poem vaguely mirrors the parallelism of Hebrew poetry. The problem is that, unlike Hebrew poetry, it has the effect of blurring differences and similarities rather than making them clear, transforming the poem into a soup of adjectives and nouns. Ginsberg offers a mushy equation of sex and peace and spirituality rather than a meaningful comparison of distinct things.

This happens again and again in his work, but it's not just Ginsberg's syntax that's repetitive. The reader who finds Ginsberg's phrase "machinery of night" in "Howl" to be wonderfully original will be disappointed to find the construction sprinkled throughout his *Collected Poems*. We have "Machinery of mass electrical dream," "machinery of a new toilet," "frail machinery," "great machinery," "remote control machinery," "milk-house machinery," and "city machinery," among many others. There may be "Robot apartments" in "Howl," but elsewhere there are also "robot ravings," "robot faces," "robot signals," "Robot towers," "illustrious robots," "robot obsession" "robot sofas," "robot proliferation," "Robot airfields," "robot pumps," "robot glove boxes," and "robot drones," again among others.

A favorite noun of Ginsberg's is "meat." In "Howl," we have "meat trucks." That might sound strangely perverse at first, but the phrase loses its punch as we encounter a "clock of meat," "mad meat," "Saintly Meat," "meat-phantom," "ganja meats," "Meat God," "meat hand," "meat-nest," "Maya-meat," "meat walls," "family meat," "meat throne," as well as other "meat-trucks."

Or there is "vibrating"—a favorite adjective of Ginsberg's, perhaps unsurprisingly, that refers to the movement of the universe, the song of poetry, and other movements. In "Howl," trees vibrate, but in other poems, so does the cosmos (repeatedly), meter, geometrical planes, trucks, cheekbones, machines, "foreign mercy," dollar bills, dashboards, and a copper kettledrum. Even a phrase like "eyeball kicks," which is almost universally associated with "Howl," was used a year earlier in "Over Kansas."

Sometimes the metaphors make sense. Other times, they are an end in themselves, and, freed of any obligation to be meaningful, they are the easiest things to create. Sex, of course, is in high relief in "Howl," as it is in Ginsberg's other poems. A particular word for male genitalia—not including its cognates—appears 104 times over five hundred poems. Instances of sex acts are too numerous to count. Bodily fluids spring eternal.

The accumulated effect of all of this, however, is not shock but a numbing boredom. After reading a certain number of Ginsberg's poems, you can almost predict, as with some Hollywood films, when it will shock our bourgeois sensibilities. Can you be avant-garde and so unintentionally predictable? A question for the ages.

Every writer has a limited bag of tricks. Henry James has his ornate sentences. Frank O'Hara, his proper nouns. Joyce, his parataxis. The problem with Ginsberg's tricks is that they don't work, or not anymore, or, if they still do, only partially. The point of his poems is to shock us to some political-spiritual-sexual realization that everything is one. What they do instead, at best, is create a vague sense, to borrow Rachel Zucker's words, that Ginsberg is "dangerous" and "hot." But he's not. This is the problem with a purely subversive poetry. Once the revolution has been won, it's not worth reading anymore—if it ever was.

All of these missteps are repeated in *Wait Till I'm Dead*, though there are some shorter concrete poems that show Ginsberg's real talent at capturing a mood or feeling indirectly—poems like "On Farm" (1973). The volume also makes obvious Ginsberg's pederasty, unfortunately. He had claimed that his affiliation with the notorious North American Man-Boy Love Association in the 1980s was in support of free speech. A handful of poems in *Wait Till I'm Dead*, which are more explicit on this score than anything in his twelve-hundred-page *Collected Poems*, would suggest otherwise.

There is a Ginsberg who is worth reading, but what he needs is a volume of poems about half the size of the current 480-page *Selected Poems*—very *selective* selected poems, and not more uncollected poetry, of which there is apparently still a good amount. The title of the present volume comes from a letter in which Ginsberg wrote: "Want more poems? Wait till I'm dead." He should have said "Go to Hell."

18

Cracks in Language

WHEN I MET JOHN Ashbery in 2005, he seemed to have difficulty remembering his time in 1950s New York with fellow poets Frank O'Hara and Kenneth Koch, which is what the roughly two dozen people in the university seminar room mostly wanted to talk about. They had read about those early days spent in artists' studios sipping martinis or at the Cedar Tavern arguing about poetry while Jackson Pollock got drunk. They had read the work, too—work that was announced as "the new American poetry" in Donald Allen's 1960 anthology by the same name and that, along with that of poets from San Francisco and Black Mountain, promised freedom from old concerns about concision and coherence.

The era had the aura of myth, especially for precocious middle-class kids from Midwestern suburbs, and here was one of only two surviving members of the New York school of poets—which included Barbara Guest and James Schuyler in addition to O'Hara, Koch, and Ashbery—unable or simply unwilling to say much about it, foxing his way out of an answer. Guest died in 2006. On September 3, 2017, Ashbery joined her at the age of ninety.

Ashbery, of course, had been foxing his whole life. Born in 1927, he was raised on a fruit farm in western New York near Lake Ontario. He disliked rural life, was uninterested in sports, and got along poorly with his father, who had a short temper. He spent much of his time reading books at his grandparents' house near Rochester, where his grandfather taught physics at the university. With the help of a neighbor who apparently recognized his promise, he attended Deerfield Academy and went on to study at Harvard, graduating cum laude in 1949.

It was at Harvard that Ashbery met O'Hara and Koch, who shared his interest in surrealism, atonality in music, and avant-garde theater. In 1952, he attended a performance of John Cage's Music of Changes and was inspired. "It was just arbitrary bangs on the piano over quite a long period of time," he told Michael H. Miller in the *Observer* in 2013. "I had been in a drought with my writing. I felt I hadn't written anything good in almost a year. It really gave me ideas about how to write poetry again."

But there was really only one idea: to use seemingly arbitrary fragments of varying diction to create poems that lacked any controlling image or narrative. Over thirty volumes of verse, several volumes of translations, and a handful of plays, Ashbery would single-mindedly explore the surface of language.

In 1954, W. H. Auden was unable to pick a winner for the Yale Series of Younger Poets; none of the manuscripts he reviewed that year seemed worthy of the prize. For the next year's competition, he picked Ashbery's poems—but apparently only begrudgingly. Some of the editors involved in the competition, who had eliminated Ashbery's submission, were outraged by the selection, and Auden wrote an ambivalent foreword warning Ashbery of the "problem" of manufacturing "calculated oddities." Other than a defensive review of *Some Trees* in *Poetry* in 1957 by Ashbery's friend O'Hara, the response to the volume was universally negative. "I could make very little headway in understanding Mr. John Ashbery's *Some Trees*," wrote William Arrowsmith in the *Hudson Review*. "Apart from two or three poems . . . I have no idea most of the time what Mr. Ashbery is talking about . . . beyond the communication of an intolerable vagueness that looks as if it was meant for precision." This judgment was typical.

But for Ashbery it was contemporary poetry that was odd and imprecise. He would go on to write poems that were even more disconnected. "My poetry," he once remarked, "imitates or reproduces the way knowledge or awareness come to me, which is by fits and starts and by indirection. I don't think poetry arranged in neat patterns would reflect that situation. My poetry is disjunct, but then so is life."

He would move to Paris in 1955 and remain there for a decade, publishing *The Tennis Court Oath* in 1962 and *Rivers and Mountains* in 1966. His break would come with the publication in 1975 of *Self-Portrait in a Convex Mirror*. It seems Ashbery had not changed, but literary tastes had:

The book won all three of America's most prestigious literary prizes—the Pulitzer, the National Book Award, and the National Book Critics Circle Award. The volume, which takes its title from the painting by Parmigianino, shows Ashbery's preoccupation with diction and syntax over meaning.

The disjunction of life could be, in Ashbery's hands, corny, terrifying, or beautiful—or simply a fact that, like all facts, becomes more interesting and harder to pin down the longer one thinks about it. "All things are palpable, none are known," he writes in "Poem in Three Parts": "The day fries, with a fine conscience, / Shadows, ripples, underbrush, old cars."

In later volumes, Ashbery would allow himself a little more fun, poking a few good-humored holes in "poetic" diction and our preoccupation with meaning. Yet our attempts to make sense of experience were never occasions for derision for Ashbery. William Logan writes that he transformed "insouciant nonsense into a charming anti-literary manner," which may be putting it a little too lightly. Still, Ashbery nudges and prods, often including himself in the great—if also serious—joke of the cosmos. His eye for cracks in the surface of language and ear for the way diction and metaphor patch the surface were the result of a lifetime of practice.

Whether or not Ashbery's work will "survive the severe judgment of time," as his early champion Harold Bloom predicted it would, is unclear. The longing to tell stories and make sense of life (and death) may prove too powerful for even the most clever and productive poet to overcome, as those questions from university students many years ago show.

19

The Soul Is a Stranger in This World

I FIRST CAME ACROSS Franz Wright's work in graduate school. It was in Nick Halpern's class on contemporary poetry, and we read Elizabeth Bishop, Denis Johnson, Jane Kenyon, Yusef Komunyakaa, Carolyn Forché, and Wright, among others.

We didn't read Wright's latest book at the time, which would have been *Il Lit* (1998), but one of his most distinctive earlier collections, *The Night World and Word Night* (1993). The volume is vintage Wright. We have the gritty pathos, the conversational tone, the self-effacing (or self-indulging, depending on how one reads it) dark humor and the occasional aphorism. His drunk father (the poet James Wright) lurks here and there, but he does not dominate the volume. Wright's friends and girlfriend, conversations with dead poets, break in on the lament of lost childhood that has otherwise so much preoccupied Wright. Stylistically, this is the Wright of big white spaces and abbreviated phrases heavy with suffering. At times, it's almost as if the poet can barely write. "Mood-altering cloud of late autumn," he writes in "The World":

> Gray deserted street
> Place settings for one—dear visible things . . .
> The insane are right, but they're still the insane.
> While there is time let me a little belong.

A central characteristic of Wright's earlier work is the tension between confession and construction. The narrative flow of his poems is often coupled with a constrained word choice, enjambment and large spaces between lines or stanzas, sudden shifts in diction, and absurd or pathetic imagery. Similar to other "confessional" poets, Wright views the poet as a "surgeon," as he puts it in "To the Poet," who must cut up his life to save it. Drawing from René Char's practice of "enlèvement-embellissement" ["removing-embellishing/beautifying"], Wright cuts words, adds spaces, shifts diction, surprises with absurd, pathetic, or startlingly beautiful images or metaphors to build something beautiful out of his suffering—to create poems that have, as he puts it, a "mysterious commonplace." For the earlier Wright, the salvation that poetry offered was at best temporary. It created a momentary community, perhaps, and provided relief from loneliness, but it was always unable to overcome that loneliness.

A lot changed from his early to later work, and a lot didn't. Following a period of institutionalization, Wright converted to Catholicism in 1999 (though he was not baptized until 2003). Hope and joy, which had until then been almost entirely absent from his poetry, quietly announced themselves first in *The Beforelife* (2000), then on the first page of *Walking to Martha's Vineyard* (2003):

>   I was standing
>   on a northern corner.
>   Moonlit winter clouds the color of the desperation of wolves.
>   Proof
>   of Your existence? There is nothing
>   but.

Wright's coyness, as the final lines demonstrate, remained, as did his unflinching honesty, his interest in the downtrodden, and his preoccupation with his father. Wright also continued in more or less the same style—the white space, the surprise breaks, the sudden shifts in diction. But the silence of these white spaces is no longer heavy with a certain darkness, as in *The Night World and Word Night*, but became the "silence" of God out of which God nevertheless speaks and comforts—a theme Wright took up in *God's Silence* (2006), his follow-up volume to the Pulitzer Prize-winning *Walking to Martha's Vineyard*.

Wright began to speak of poetry as a sacrament. Poetry's redemptive potential, it turns out, is a reflection of Christ's redemption, not a replacement of it, as it was for Rilke. The near despair expressed in previous volumes is transformed in his later work. "There is hope in the past," Wright writes in "I for One": "I am so glad // there is no fear, / and finally I can // ask no second life."

In his last three volumes—*Wheeling Motel* (2009), *Kindertotenwald* (2011), and *F* (2013)—Wright returned to his childhood in part, while at the same time continuing to explore his faith, but with a shift in style in *Kindertotenwald*. Mostly gone (though not entirely) are the white spaces and constraint. Instead, we have big block—sometimes surreal—paragraphs. Block after block text can be off-putting, but *Kindertotenwald* is a pleasure. The poems themselves are some of Wright's most varied in terms of subject matter. We have folk tales, vignettes of Nietzsche, Verlaine, Basho, Saint Teresa, Kierkegaard, and other unidentified voices.

These voices often long for some communion with others. "On My Father's Farm in New York City," for example, begins: "In the yard it is just getting light, as they say, and I wish I could meet them sometime and shake hands. I have been waiting all night for this, here by the one window, enthroned in his absence." In other poems, such as in "As Was," it is the speaker who is responsible for his own isolation: "You may be the beast right now but one day, rest assured, of something you are going to be the gory feast. Take me. The arrow found me in the end, one I myself had so long ago blindly let fly, what the hell was I thinking?" In "Deep Revision," the poet laments: "I don't want to write anything, ever. I just want you."

This takes us back to one of Wright's earlier preoccupation with the power of poetry to heal human loneliness. As in *The Night World and Word Night*, poetry fails to heal the wounds others inflict on us and the wounds we inflict on ourselves. In "The Last Person in Purgatory," Wright writes: "Company! But nothing happens, of course, that was all over with long ago, there remains no one but me, me with my tiny bat wings that don't work." And yet, unlike in *The Night World and Word Night*, poetry's failure does not lead to despair in *Kindertotenwald*. In "Song," the penultimate poem in the volume, Wright, perhaps addressing himself, writes: "Are you finished debating the blind who insist that light doesn't exist, and have proof of it? Nobody's alone, God is alone. If you liked being born, you'll love dying."

I'd quibble with "God is alone." After all, if our capacity for community did not come from the Trinity, where did it come from? God is alone and not alone at the same time. His point, however, if not in this particular poem but in his work from at least *The Beforelife*, is that while human poetry cannot save, God's can.

The central piece in *F* is "Entries of the Cell," a long poem in which Wright, who was diagnosed with cancer in 2008, considers his life and work, death, and the afterlife. The poem is dedicated to the poet Fady Joudah, whose *Textu* (2013) is a collection of cell phone poems each with stanzas exactly 160 characters long—the character limit of the software Joudah used to write the poems. There are no such arbitrary constraints in Wright's long poem, which also contains the only reference to the title of the volume: "And look what I've come across in the middle of these disintegrating / pages. // It's a capital *F* that takes up the whole page. // My name, or grade in life?" The appearance of the first letter of his name, created by the lines of poetry, may, indeed, have been an accident, but it is one that is particularly relevant to the central argument of the poem. According to Wright, we have been deluded by narcissism and materialism. We are infatuated with ourselves. We disregard the suffering of others and view love as an illusion. The only thing we view as real, Wright suggests, is animal suffering, which was his own view, in part, before he came to Christ:

> Then I remembered how long long ago I had bought it, the
> whole illusion, everything from the most
> remote star to the bubble of time that will burst
> before I can finish this phrase; everything from
> the small bloody scream of our first appearance
> to our speechless and forsaken exit. All will be
> forgotten, everything you perceived, thought,
> dreamed, hoped, remembered, . . . all the past

As Wright suggests here, this belief in the meaningless of the universe is itself a yearning for a sort of salvation—one in which "all the past," all the suffering will be forgotten. The rub, of course, is that it requires the annihilation of all that is human: "Show me the first to form / words, the first to weep, the first to sing. The / first to kill no others but himself. The first to / die for someone else." True salvation begins when one recognizes that love is "Of all things least illusory."

Nobody does love and joy better in poetry—and perhaps worse in life—than Wright. He, of course, had his fair share of public outbursts. There was the back and forth with William Logan in 2006 and, more recently, his angry complaints about MFA poetry on Facebook. This shows up a little in these later volumes, too. In "Märchen," for example, from *Kindertotenwald*, Wright imagines a "Prince" and his "Mrs." who "become hopelessly lost in the forest and apply to several minor writing programs."

In Wright's defense, his antagonism toward MFA programs seemed to me to be mostly an expression of his love for poetry and his frustration at how some—by no means all—MFA programs have turned poetry into a technique that is less about art and more about getting a first book publication and a tenure-track job at another university. It has been bad for *risk* in art, and Wright is not the only one to have suggested so.

In his poems, however, he has nothing but compassion for the unnamed homeless, the addict in the corner of a gutted building, and strangers walking down the street infected by loneliness. And regarding joy, we have lines like:

> Here am I, Lord,
> sitting on a suitcase,
> waiting for my train.
> The sun is shining.
> I'm never coming back.

It was phrases similar to these in *Walking to Martha's Vineyard* that set Logan off. He wrote at the time that they were no different from the "kitschy sanctimoniousness that puts nodding Jesus dolls on car dashboards." Joy is offensive, and it can look like "kitschy sanctimoniousness," especially when a poet does not give a little wink and nod to a knowing skepticism that excludes feelings such as this as impossibly false from the get-go.

Logan's point, and rightly so, is that it's the poet's job to make language *work*. The question is *for whom*. I think many readers of Wright, myself included, are attracted to his work in part because these blunt and at times embarrassingly happy lines are not found anywhere else in contemporary poetry. It is a refreshing respite from the hedged hand-me-down Ashberian surrealism of Stevenesque doubt.

This is not to say that it always works in Wright. In "Crumpled-up Note Blowing Away," for example, the pathos gets a little out of control: "But I've said all that / I had to say," he writes, "In writing. / I signed my name. / It's death's move." Except he hadn't said all he has had to say in writing—at least at that point (he died in 2015)—and it's always death's move. The additional periods here have the effect of making these lines more dramatic than they can or should be in this particular context. It just doesn't work. But I'll take these sorts of missteps for lines like this: "I am standing alone with everyone else at the center of the world, / a violet ray of noon piercing my forehead. / And all at once it is the middle of the night."

Concision, pacing, the juxtaposition of absurd or striking images and direct speech are all used by Wright to capture something of what it means—what it feels like—to be "a stranger in this world." And few poets writing today do this better than Wright. He died in 2015, and there is no one at present who matches his startling honesty.

20

John Updike's Occasional Verse

THAT JOHN UPDIKE WROTE poems as well as novels is news to few people who follow contemporary poetry. Before his death, a common view of Updike's poetry was that it was light, entertaining stuff that he wrote to refresh himself after the serious work of fiction. After his death, however, a number of critics have hailed it as the elephant in the room of contemporary American poetry. In his review of *Endpoint* for *The New York Times*, for example, Clive James writes that while Updike did not write much poetry, a single poem ("Bird Caught in My Deer Netting") proves "that he not only had the whole tradition of English-language poetry in his head, he had the means to add to it." For Michael Dirda of *The Washington Post*, Updike hits his "Mortal Mark" in the collection.

Critics tend to demonize the living and glorify the dead. There is a little bit of the latter going on in James's review in particular. If we ignore the hyperbole, however, his main point—that Updike was indeed a serious poet, albeit a minor one because of the relative sparseness of his poetry—is correct. Yet, it seems to me, James fails to identify the right domain of Updike's accomplishment. He hangs his hat on the few "serious" poems that exhibit "all the linguistic vigour of the prose that had made his novels compulsory reading." This is misplaced to the extent that it dismisses Updike's light verse and occasional poems, and it is in these poems that Updike's true poetic accomplishment is found.

Technically, the term "occasional" refers to poems written for a specific, often official, occasion. There is a sense, however, in which all art is occasional. All art is grounded in the particularities of human experience.

This is one of the things that makes art *art* and not philosophy. For Sir Philip Sidney, for example, poetry embodies virtues and vices in finite situations. It does not define love in the abstract. It shows us what love looks like. For Rainer Maria Rilke, poetry names objects of experience—"house, / bridge, well, gate"—and provides them with a fullness of being; for Boris Pasternak, poetry is an expression of what life feels like "now." Even Wallace Stevens, who stated that poetry "must be abstract," cannot escape the particularities of his experience. His poems are full of things—snow, blackbirds, oranges—and sounds.

Yet, while certain poets embrace the "occasional" nature of artistic expression, including the everyday, others wish to escape it altogether and express disdain for the light, naive verse of the "everyday" poets. No doubt a lot of sentimental, metered prose wrongly passes for poetry today. But so too does a lot of obfuscation. If "difficult" poetry is the natural result of a powerful mind examining the complex problems of the world, it can have other less noble, less intellectually compelling sources, as well.

One of those sources, as Czeslaw Milosv argues in "Against Incomprehensible Poetry," is the rejection of the personal and transcendent God of Christianity and the rise of the poet as a priest or prophet of Art. Following the work of the French Symbolists, certain poets produced inscrutable texts to both create and confirm their superior position above the masses. Understood in this way, poetry does not represent the longings, fears, virtues, and vices of the human mind but gives form to the primordial, hitherto unexpressed "force" at work in the world. These forms can, in turn, be scrutinized for their residue of "spiritual sentiment," to use Georges Braque's term. This effort, Milosv argues, quoting Ortega y Gasset, entailed a "dehumanization of art"—a movement away from drama, emotion, and feeling and toward radical formal experimentation.

Whether Milosv is correct or not regarding the influence of Symbolism, there is no doubt that there has been a "dehumanization of art." If for the Symbolists the poet was a priest, today he is a grammarian. Having rejected the notion of a transcendent, moral God, a number of modern scientists and artists reduce human nature to its constituent parts. Consequently, the material of the lyric—love, virtue, vice, and all other "qualia"— are reduced to the firings of neurons. This often leaves the poet little choice but to use what is left of meaning in language to create puns, jokes, and wordplays by the tossing of a coin.

John Updike's Occasional Verse

It is against this "dehumanization of art" that Updike's occasional poetry can, in part, be understood. Without overstating the case, the treatment of everyday situations and objects of which the "I" of the poet is the center can be understood as an effort to maintain a sense of self. Faced by the attacks of a secularized modern science against all that is human, Updike's occasional poems and light verse function as a "testament of the self," to borrow Frank O'Hara's term, rightly pointing to the irreducibility of human emotions and feeling while, at the same time, highlighting the self's multiple and seemingly inescapable contradictions.

Updike's *Endpoint* is full of the finite particulars of modern existence. In the long title poem, which begins on the poet's birthday in 2002 and ends the month before his death, Updike charts his attachment to the material world—an attachment that is both exhilarating and disappointing, powerful and fleeting. The final line of the opening section of the poem states the central motif of the volume: "Birthday, death day—what day is not both?" Everywhere the poet looks—from Connecticut winters, news of Payne Stewart's death, and malls in Tucson to the architecture of St. Petersburg and thunderstorms in Vermont—he is reminded of both the fullness of life and its impermanence. The arthritis of his left hand reminds him of his hand's relatively leisurely life compared to that of his right and the irony that it must be the first to suffer the foretaste of death. He recalls how Frankie Laine's voice in the sweet shop of his youth "soared, assuring us of finding our / desire," which, of course, would be both fulfilled and unfilled. The expanse and silence of snow is both peaceful and frightening, and the golden leaves are both strikingly beautiful and dead, piled up "demanding disposal."

One of the ironies, however, of establishing the contours of feeling is that as one's sense of self increases, death becomes all the more unbearable. In one section, the poet is in a plane, and as he gains altitude and is removed from the "Raw days" of winter, the world below him loses its distinction. All the houses are white. Golf courses and woods become like rivers and the sea. Yet, as the plane descends and the world gains in detail—"Manhattan's spine" first becomes visible, followed rapidly by "Riverside cathedral"—fear grips the poet: "We seem too low, my palms begin to sweat." It is this fear, brought on by the sudden detail of the world, with which Updike struggles throughout the book. Death, he writes, "is real, and dark, and huge."

However, rather than escape this fear via abstraction (which is, perhaps, another source of obfuscation in poetry), he confronts it head on, names it with all the detail his mind can summon, and, in the end, turns to the faith of his childhood, repeating the words of Psalm 23: "Surely goodness and mercy shall follow me all the days of my life," to which he adds "my life, forever." Like Saint Augustine, perhaps, so with Updike: The restlessness of youth, of Rabbit, is replaced with a hope to inherit that final rest, that fullness of existence forever.

Thus, while light verse and occasional poems can be just that—light and occasional—in the work of most poets, in the hands of the best poets, and Updike is perhaps one of them, they become the tools of serious philosophical, ethical, and even theological work. If, as Geoffrey Hill claims, the poet's excavation of the obscure meanings of words is a means of pointing us toward that "terrible aboriginal calamity," so, too, does Updike's use of words point us toward what is everywhere obvious, but often ignored—that life is both a "passionate sweetness" and a "desolation," evoking both dreams of the afterlife in "Acres of gold leaf, feathered into place" and nightmares of a never-ending death.

21

Scott Cairns and the Promise of a Future Fullness

SOME POETS ARE PREOCCUPIED with a single question, and Scott Cairns is one of them. Despite the breadth of his *Collected Poems*, a big volume that includes a selection of juvenilia and previously uncollected poems along with everything from his books to date, Cairns regularly turns to the question of *faithful* language. How can we speak truthfully about ourselves and the world, and how can we speak truthfully about God?

For Cairns, one answer—among others—is to be a little sexy. Surprised? Welcome to Scott Cairns's world. The first poem of the volume (after an address to the reader) is "Taking Off Our Clothes." "Let's pretend," Cairns writes, "for now there is no such thing / as metaphor; you know, waking up will just / be waking up, darkness will no longer have to be / anything but dark; this could all be happening / in Kansas." And "taking off our clothes" would also be just that:

> We'd have nice blue sheets and a wool blanket
> for later. I could be the man and you could be
> the woman. We'd talk about real things, casually
> and easily taking off our clothes. We would be
> naked and would hold onto each other a long time,
> talking, saying things that would make us
> grin. We'd laugh off and on, all the time
> unconcerned with things like breath, or salty
> skin, or the way our gums show when we really
> smile big. After a little while, I'd get you a glass of water.

It may sound odd for a poet to wish—if only momentarily—that there's "no such thing / as metaphor," but metaphors can be troublesome things. They simultaneously contain more meaning than we need and narrow it. When we use words like "morning" and "wake," Cairns writes in "Waking in the Borrowed House," "we fool ourselves / by thinking we've imagined all / we say," or we imagine that by naming "the sun lifting past the ridge" we have "given a word / to contain it."

Metaphors can also lie. "We say *flight of the imagination*," Cairns writes in "Idiot Psalm 9," "but stand ankle deep in silt. We say *deep / life of the mind*, but seal the stone to keep / the tomb untouched." We are dying, Cairns writes in "Another Elegy," and "dying want / some words for setting down"—that is, we both need and lack them.

The temptation is to see the failure of language as proof that the world is meaningless and to welcome an early death, whose definitive simplicity offers an apparent freedom from our "vague mistakes." "We have stories," Cairns writes in "The Adulterer," "full of unclear language, whole volumes / of wrong names. Each time we find the place / where we can stand our vague mistakes no longer, / we settle into what will pass as sleep." This is the temptation Hamlet faces in his famous soliloquy on suicide, and Keats in "To Sleep."

For Cairns, however, this failure of language offers hope. The "limit" of poetry is a "proof" of some possible future presence. It offers "a hint of what words might do," he writes in "Impressions," "a taste / of real light and a world of whole men" Or as he puts it in "Articulation": "If, one / fresh morning, I should come to apprehend / how ever full with presence every breath / now is—and even now—I have a sense / my words would grow so heavy as to still. / I suppose that morning then would open / to our eighth day, whose sunrise will not set." While language is "never exact" and meaning always slips, the temporary presence that poetry creates is a promise of a future fullness.

So what does this have to do with sex? Well, sex is one thing that proves that metaphors do actually point to something. In fact, Cairns argues, sex is a metaphor, which is why in the opening poem the poet can pretend to ignore others. Sex is "the sudden speech of two as one," Cairns writes in "Ode: Erotic World," its intimate language "most engaged, most attentive to / the mystery engraved in this / our common body, blessed with both // the pulse of animality / and Spirit's animating breath." Sex reminds us of our true selves—of our dual nature—as animals created in the image of God, but it also embodies love. In this sense, it gives us a glimpse of the presence that poetry always points toward but never captures.

If this is the case, one of the tasks of the poet is to avoid contributing to "pretty . . . fictions" that dull our ability to perceive this partially expressed presence—whether these are the fictions of a theology that leaves no space for mystery or those of Wallace Stevens, for example, whose theory of poetry as a "supreme fiction" transforms art into a mere diversion that, for all Stevens's own verbal virtuosity, can sometimes be oddly dogmatic and predictable. According to Cairns, the poet is to "taste and feel" the "vertiginous / assemblage" of "keen articulations" while at the same time recognizing that "full / none of which quite seems to satisfy." This requires a commitment to a *clear* ambiguity, a perceptible doubleness, and it is why so many of Cairns's poems, like Stevens's, with whom he shares both a great deal and very little, seem to turn on a single word.

It's also the task of the poet, paradoxically, to lead us to silence. The end of art, for Cairns, is to force us to face the mystery of a transcendent God who speaks. In the playfully titled "And Yet Another Page and Yet," Cairns asks: "What to make of this collision— / of cluttered mind and cluttered shore?" His answer: "I made not great conclusion, save / to shed my walking gear and swim." For the Orthodox Cairns, the practice of silence (as well as that of *living*, properly understood) offers a respite from our "roiling confusion" because it is one of poetry's proper ends.

Another answer to the question of how to speak *faithfully* is to speak with a good measure of compassion for human frailty and humor. Cairns regularly addresses the poor and neglected in his work, because the poor are so clearly *here* and because our natural bent is, wrongly, to ignore them. This is, again, part of Cairns's poetics of testament, but it's also a moral act that calls us to acknowledge the unhappy state and weakness that we share with those less fortunate. In "Infirmities," he writes that "the way the blind boy / laughs when he stumbles / makes you laugh with him some mornings. / Some mornings it hurts to see." Faithful poetry helps us to *see* the boy and ourselves, however much this might hurt. Put another way, if the poor, as Cairns writes in "Blesséd," "have no effectual recourse against / the blithe designs of the rich," one of the purposes of poetry is to become the voice of the "mute" and "maligned."

Of course, this does not mean that Cairns is a heavy-handed moralist—far from it. One of the pleasures of his work is his observation that our intellectual limits and physical weakness are pretty funny in the divine scheme of things. Our pilgrimage to self-knowledge, to a proper silence facing our Creator, and to love for our fellow human beings is a slow one indeed—hence the title of Cairns's collected poems—but it's also a comedy of errors, both of our own making and others'.

This comic touch is present throughout Cairns's work but particularly so in his *Idiot Psalms*. In "Idiot Psalm 2," Cairns asks God, the "Shaper of varicolored clay and cellulose, O Keeper / of same, O Subtle Tweaker, Agent / of energies both appalling and unobserved," to keep him "sufficiently limber that I might continue / to enjoy my morning run among the lilies / and the rowdy waterfowl, that I might / delight in this and every evening's intercourse / with the woman You have set beside me," and that he might "awaken daily" with "a giddy joy, / the idiot's undying expectation, / despite the evidence." And in "Idiot Psalm 7," he complains, somewhat more seriously:

> And lo, the fraught perplexities accrue,
> collude, compound, and hasten to compose
> before us now and, yea, extending far
> as we might squint into the distance
> ***
> The aging Labrador's stiff leg won't
> let her climb the stair. Our neighbor's late
> C-section has brought fresh heartbreak home.
> I swear the very air smells of tar or creosote, maybe
> tire rubber burning. The game ball's rolled
> clean off the court. A little help!

The ball may have rolled off the court of our lives, but it hasn't in *Collected Poems*. Cairns's precision and whimsy regularly break through our petty defenses to teach us something about ourselves and our Maker. This is the name of the game, and Scott Cairns can play.

22

Paul Lake and the Politics of Language

THE TITLE POEM OF Paul Lake's *The Republic of Virtue* begins like Genesis. "In Year One," he writes, "the month of *Vintage*, time began." Instead of the Spirit of God hovering over the waters, "Fog hovered above the earth, like an emanation / Of spirits underground." What follows, however, is a retelling of Robespierre's France after the Revolution—the so-called Republic of Virtue whose goal was to throw off the shackles of a "tyrannical" Christian morality and replace it with "liberty and equality." Instead, Robespierre renamed vice virtue, associated terror with justice, and executed dissenters in the guise of defending freedom:

> "Revolutions, my friend, are not made out of rosewater,"
> Cried Danton, as The Committee of Public Safety
> Sent spies among the crowd to sniff complaints.
> Addressing fellow citizens as "Ladies"
> Could lead to steps where other traps were sprung
> And heads sent rolling. "If virtue be the spring
> Of government in peace," roared Robespierre,
> "The spring of government in revolution
> Is virtue joined with terror. . . ." In *Thermidor*,
> The month of heat, his words rolled to their term
> Among piled corpses. Women doused the ground
> With rosewater, as choirs of children cheered,
> Rags pressed against their mouths to blunt the odor.

Lake's skillful skewering of Robespierre's hubris and the Revolution's misguided attempt to remake society is both elegant and powerful. The Republic's hypocrisy would be almost comical if it weren't also true.

But the poem also reminds us that France, recently terrorized for its freedom of speech, once terrorized those who opposed its definition of freedom. This should in no way temper condemnation of the *Charlie Hebdo* murders. But it should discourage simplistic dichotomies and jingoisms. France and the United States have a high view of freedom and tolerance, but as this poem and the rest of Lake's volume shows, that commitment is not always as unwavering as we like to think.

One of Lake's preoccupations is the use of language to deceive or confuse. In "Epilogue to 'The Emperor's New Clothes,'" a poem in which Lake recasts the classic fairy tale in modern times, the Emperor appoints one of the charlatan weavers as his "Minister of Information" to spin "Transparent fictions into lines / And patterns to clothe royal sins / And cloak imperial designs" on the nightly news. The other becomes a "tenured chair" and "employs his language games / To show what lies beneath all texts / Is nothingness."

In Lake's view, relativism, coupled with a "critical theory" whose goal is to undermine meaning itself, are the enemies of community and tolerance despite presenting themselves as champions of difference. In reality, these two forces demonize difference and gnaw at the threads of the cooperation needed for complex societies to flourish. In "Intolerance: A Memo," for example, Lake writes, "Hate means whatever public voices say; / Inflaming first the hater, then the hated, // It spreads whenever ideas are debated / That might cause some discomfort or dismay." And in "Allegory of Bees," he writes:

> Affectless drones, observing the wild dance
> Of honey-drudgers, smile with condescension
> At the ecstatic mass's naive notion
> That waggled steps can measure a straight course
> To hidden nectar, or unplotted land
> Be spanned and mapped by buzzing blurring signs,
> While honey-drudgers leave in steady lines,
> Tracking the legend to its honeyed source.

In "A Language Game," Lake turns Gertrude Stein's remark that "A rose is a rose is a rose" on its head. While "skeptics claim," Lake writes, that

"All words are null and void," the end result of this idea is to make "only skeptics, trapped in sentencing, [. . .] null and void." Critical theory, Lake suggests, will destroy itself, like the Ouroboros, but perhaps only after causing irreparable damage.

This does not mean that Lake espouses a simplistic view of language or poetry. Poetry is an object, shaped by its own sound and meaning, that also reflects the mind and the material world. It is neither an autonomous artifact nor a mere mirror. In "Echoes," Lake imagines a dolphin "bored with his one-sided conversation / With ocean floors and passing schools of fish" turning to "higher forms of mimicry." He "imitates his own returning wave / With cunningly cast measures that behave / To dolphin ears like carvings by Bernini, / Transforming shoal and branching coral reef / To frozen arias of sculpted sound."

For Lake, the abuse of language is not limited to plutocrats or fat academics at elite institutions. In fact, it often begins in smaller, initially powerless groups looking to reshape society to their advantage. In "End of the Road," he writes:

> When all roads led to Rome,
> unRoman ways
> made inroads
> into Rome
> so Rome's ways changed.
> Now when strangers go
> to Rome,
> to do what Romans do,
> neither they
> nor Romans know
> what Romans do, to do,
> some even deeming
> it unRoman
> they once knew.

Other poems deal more directly with the war of cultures or nations, and the sad fact that violence and terrorism show no signs of ending any time soon. In "Lessons from Gaza," Lake retells the story of Samson and asks, "What is the moral of this tale?" "What else," he writes, "but that, when building nations, / To nurse a grudge for generations; / To preface slaughter with a prayer; / To jawbone foes when weapons fail; / To stand apart while losing jackals; / To catch your foes packed into temples / Or market squares and kill wholesale."

The volume isn't all politics and satire, however. The first section contains a number of lyrics touching on the family, and there is a selection of poems on the craft of poetry. In "Home Free," for example, Lake addresses a teenage daughter who storms out of the house in "adolescent pique." "At first, I spurn the bait," he writes,

> And watch the clock and phone
> With feigned indifference,
> Refusing to succumb
> To scenes imagination
> Plays on its lurid screen,
> Till out of patience and
> Heart climbing in my throat,
> I grab my keys, cell phone,
> And hit the empty street
> To track your shadow down
> Among the leafy shades
> And mildly spreading lawns
> Of our small Southern town.

The daughter is found, but she refuses to return home, "However much I chide, / or threaten and cajole." As the speaker watches his daughter walk away, "the truth strikes home— / That you're not mine to keep." Another poem is a prayer for a father much diminished by age and dementia. "*Please*," Lake writes,

> *Let wings take him up now to the ballroom of heaven*
> *As a brassy young boy he took up the horn.*
> *Let him trumpet the tunes that wooed his young wife.*
> *Make melody again. Dance the jitterbug of joy.*

Among other things, these bittersweet poems on family life—and, in particular, on miscommunication within the family—show that the bond of blood and of a shared name and place form a community that is the basis for all other communities, however imperfect. Societies that turn on the family or on language itself are attacking the very foundation of their own existence.

Erudite, wise, and, most importantly, never boring, *The Republic of Virtue* possesses a simple elegance that is both entirely natural and startling. It is one of the richest books of poetry in recent years and shows Lake to be one of our best poets.

23

A. E. Stallings's Practiced Movements

IN THE SECOND POEM of A. E. Stallings's penultimate collection, *Olives*, we have her poetics in miniature. "Jigsaw Puzzle" closes with that universal experience of puzzling—the missing final piece:

> Slowly you restore
> The fractured world and start
> To re-create an afternoon before
> It fell apart:
>
> Here is summer, here is blue,
> Here two lovers kissing,
> And here the nothingness shows through
> Where one piece is missing.

The four corners of the puzzle become in Stallings's poetry four-line stanzas (her preferred stanza length) in which she re-creates "afternoon" events, most often touching on domestic matters. These afternoons, while wonderfully crafted, are not mere confections, but stark reminders of life's missing pieces.

The title poem of the volume, for example, tells us that, for some reason, we crave bitterness in life, "Full of the golden past and cured in brine," as much as sweetness. "Sometimes a craving comes for salt, not sweet," Stallings writes, "For fruits that you can eat / Only if pickled in a vat of tears—." In "The Compost Heap," the haphazard care of a garden turns up the "dark glissando of a snake," and in "Two Nursery Rhymes: Lullaby and Rebuttal," we have a mother exclaim in exasperation: "For crying out loud,

A. E. Stallings's Practiced Movements

/ It's only spilt milk." These universal events of human life—eating, gardening, and caring for children—can be moments of great satisfaction, but they are also moments that are most often spoiled by sin, or, to borrow Stallings's vocabulary, by "nothingness" and "shadow."

It is not insignificant that the volume is broken into four sections, beginning with "The Argument" and ending with "Fairy-Tale Logic." If philosophy tries to find the missing piece of the world, poetry reminds us, it seems for Stallings, that certain pieces will always remain missing. In "Fairy-Tale Logic," for example, she begins with the observation that "Fairy tales are full of impossible tasks: / Gather the chin hairs from a man-eating goat, / Or cross a sulfuric lake in a leaky boat." "You have to believe," she writes coyly,

> That you have something impossible up your sleeve—
> The language of snakes, perhaps; an invisible cloak,
> An army of ants at your back, or a lethal joke,
> The will to do whatever must be done;
> Marry a monster. Hand over your firstborn son.

The logic of fairy tales, in other words, is that there are no fairy tales, in the now clichéd sense of that term, at least none of our own making.

Stallings, though, is no brooding Russian. If these poems show us that life is always missing something of fullness, she does it with a sharp wit and good humor. In "Dinosaur Fever," she laments that stage of development parents loathe more than puberty:

> Dinosaur fever—they all get it.
> Kindergartners of either sex.
> It'll drive you crazy if you let it—
> Facts on *Tyrannosaurus rex*,
>
> *Triceratops, Iguanodon,*
> *Stegosaurus,* always a classic;
> You must become an expert on
> All things Cretaceous and Jurassic.
>
> Tots tell you what things mean in Greek,
> In tones superior and mammalian;
> It seems they only just learned to speak
> And now they speak sesquipedalian.

Puberty, of course, will bring its own fevers. She writes in "Pop Music" that "The music that your son will listen to / To drive you mad / Has yet to be invented. Be assured, / However, it is approaching from afar / Like the light of some Chaldean star." Yet, unlike Dinosaur fever, such music has, at least Stallings seems to hope, some real relation to love or life:

> And while you knit another ugly sweater,
> The pulsars of the brave new tunes will boom
> From the hormonal miasma of his room,
> Or maybe they'll just beam into his brain—
> Unheard melodies are better.
>
> Thus it has always been. Maybe that's why
> The sappy retro soundtrack of your youth
> Ambushes you sometimes in a café
> At this almost-safe distance, and you weep, or nearly weep
> For all you knew of beauty, or of truth.

To be honest, when I hear some song of my youth, I find myself laughing more than weeping, but maybe I'm insensitive. In any case, these somewhat lighter poems provide variety and balance to the volume.

These are also the poems of an American abroad. Stallings, who is from Decatur, Georgia, studied classics at the University of Georgia, but currently lives with her husband, John Psaropoulos, who is the editor of the English-language *Athens News*, in Athens, Greece. We have poems on visits to the countryside and to the First Cemetery of Athens, and throughout the volume there is the comingling of old and new, life and death, love and fear. In "Two Violins" the poet chooses a yellow "Baltic amber" violin from "the Old World" that is as "Light as an exile's suitcase" over a new "fire-red" piece made from "a torn-down church's pew." Unlike the red violin, which answers "merrily and clear," the yellow instrument is "sad" and mellow, responding, as if by magic, to the poet's unpracticed fingers.

Greece, perhaps, is Stallings's old violin. Her "fingers," however, at least in *Olives*, are marked by the sure, practiced movements of a master.

24

A Modern Martial

THE FIRST POEM OF A. M. Juster's second collection of mostly original verse, *Sleaze & Slander*, is "Grandmother Gives Birth to Chimp." The title, as becomes apparent, is from a tabloid. "You never know what ends up being true," Juster writes before noting a few other things that sound outrageous but could nevertheless be called true: "Amelia Earhart flew to Tumbuktu, / then on to Kansas to escape it all," "The Loch Ness Monster is quite real, though small," and "Houdini's ghost is merely overdue."

Why begin a collection of comic verse called *Slander* with a poem on truth? It's a joke, of course. Juster's tongue is firmly in cheek: "Don't cringe when cynics call us 'off the wall'!" / "Thank God the tabloids keep us on the ball!" But it's more than that. Not to be a killjoy (we'll get to the sleaze in a moment), but it's helpful to remember, since Juster is something of a Latin scholar and a Catholic, that we get "slander" from *scandalum* or "scandal." Thomas Aquinas defined *scandalum* as an evil action that leads to someone else's sin, but it can also refer to good actions that are wrongly viewed as evil. Christ is a "stumblingblock" or *skandalon*, according to the apostle Paul, to those who reject him.

The refrain "You never know" is an appropriate opening, then, to a collection that reminds us of how outrageously vindictive, proud, and lusty we can all be. Some of the poems may offend (there's a translation of the Middle Welsh "Poem of the Prick" and another I'm too Protestant to name), but they're also humorous reminders of our frailty and excess, bawdiness and bile.

The Soul Is a Stranger in This World

Juster is at his best in his short poems, which are deliciously acerbic. In "Your Midlife Crisis," the first of three epigrams "From the Workplace" (Juster is the pen name of Michael J. Astrue, who was the head of the Social Security Administration until 2013), he writes: "You found yourself, but at an awful cost. / We liked you better when you were lost." In "To My Ambitious Colleague": "Your uphill climb will never stop; / scum always rises to the top." "I kept hoping she would come alone," he writes in "Mismatch." "She's a gem, but he's a kidney stone."

As far as bawdiness goes, there's this translation of Luxorius, which Juster renders (rightly in my view) as a limerick:

> If his words could equal his penis,
> He'd be known as a legal genius.
> He is up half the night
> Missing laws he should cite
> While joined by his servant of Venus.

But there's humility, too. In "Self-portrait at Fifty," Juster writes:

> None of this can be denied:
> crabby, flabby, full of pride;
> hypertensive, pensive, snide;
> slowing, growing terrified.

In "Candid Headstone," he asks us to remember "what's left of Michael Juster": "A failure filled with bile and bluster," and in "Botches" he laments that "These half-finished poems of mine / lie in pieces on the floor / as if Doctor Frankenstein / couldn't focus on his chore."

The comparatively longer poems (roughly between ten and forty lines) touch on political and literary matters. As a long-time civil servant—and one of the good ones, according to Paul Mariani's 2010 profile of him in *First Things*—Astrue may have heard the following excuse from "Mistakes Were Made" more than once: "My people screwed up on their own; / I would have stopped them had I known." There's a Supreme Court drinking song, "A Panegyric for Presidents' Day" (which begins with the pleasantly corny "In malls today it is inhuman / Not to talk of Taft or Truman"), and "A Prayer to Bill Gates" ("We call to Thee, though Thou shalt not reply"), as well as a send-up of T. S. Eliot (an early influence), William Carlos Williams, and Wallace Stevens called "Prufrock's Thirteen Ways of Looking at a Red Wheelbarrow Glazed with Rain beside White Chickens."

The dialogue in the translation of two of Horace's satires is occasionally confusing but also refreshingly colloquial. His translation of over seventy of Martial's epigrams is nearly perfect, and matches or surpasses that of the late James Michie. He renders Epigram 28 in Book One, for example, as "To say Acerra stinks of day-old booze is wrong! / Each drink is freshened all night long!" This is much better than Walter C. A. Ker's literal translation in the Loeb ("He who fancies that Acerra reeks of yesterday's wine is wrong. Acerra always drinks till daylight") and far superior to Garry Wills' clunky and charmless "They claimed, with blamings not condign / He reeked at morn of last night's wine. / He intermits not in such ways: / Not last night's wine—it was today's").

One of my favorite original poems in the volume is "Proposed Clichés." Would that they were. "Ask not what your country can do," he writes in one, "for fear of the answer." "Love is like a hard-time sentence," he writes in another, "but better than cancer." "If you're crazy like a fox, / get tested for rabies."

This is a book for the curmudgeon, the wayward washed-up uncle, and anyone else who knows that life is messy and human beings are ridiculous and endearing. It's also for lovers of wit and anyone happy to learn from a bit of comic carnality.

25

Flarf and Form

IN THE LATE 1970S, Charles Bernstein and Bruce Andrews argued in the short-lived but influential magazine $L=A=N=G=U=A=G=E$ that the purpose of poetic form was to reveal the constructed nature of the self and confront capitalistic "oppression" by creating fragmented poems that supposedly could not be assimilated into a market economy. Instead of writing about feelings and emotions, which presumes a continuous self, Bernstein and others, notably Ron Silliman, suggested that poets use fragmentation, ellipses, parataxis, and formal randomness in order to free the reader from the false consciousness of selfhood.

There are a number of problems with this theory of poetic form. One is that it has almost without fail led to boring poems. That's the point, Bernstein might say, so as to better avoid being co-opted by the market and preserve individual freedom. The problem is that it doesn't do either of these things. James Matthew Wilson has pointed out in *The Fortunes of Poetry in an Age of Unmaking* that while the goal of cacophony, clashing images, and fragmentation in contemporary poetry is often (though not always) to undermine supposedly bourgeois conventions in the name of aesthetic, sexual, or moral freedom, what such poetry does is merely replace one set of conventions with another, kicking the unattainable can of freedom further down the road. Purists form new schools of anti-poetry to attack previous ones for failing to be radical enough only to be attacked by a younger generation themselves.

In fact, Wilson notes that the market paradoxically plays a central role in validating such work. The use of ugliness and nonsense is necessary, at least according to the contemporary Marxist conception of art, to resist "the reifying logic of modern capitalism." Wilson writes: "By refusing to be absorbed in the marketplace, art in its very uselessness and apparent ugliness enacts an isolated liberation from the 'exchange' relationships that dominate market societies." Yet such poems are published in hundreds of small literary magazines in order to signal that the poet has learned the conventions and can teach them to others in an MFA program. The poem is not meant to be read or to be performed. It exists merely to be "seen." "It is meant to indicate," Wilson writes, "that so-and-so has been published and this validates the continuation of publishing just this sort of thing." What is that but an exchange relationship?

Over the past few years, however, the elliptical lyric is rightfully, though slowly, falling out of fashion. This is a good sign, but if poetry is to regain its cultural purchase, it must excavate the ideological roots of the elliptical lyric and return to an understanding of poetic form as a reflection of the natural order, which is something slower in coming (or, more accurately, to which we have been slow to return).

A recent series on poetry by Adam Roberts at *The Atlantic* is a case in point. While I appreciate Roberts' effort to avoid writing a blanket eulogy for contemporary poetry, his suggestion that "Flarf" has the potential to reconnect with readers following the demise of "elliptical" poetry is deeply flawed.

Flarf is poetry composed from the results of Google and Twitter searches. And unlike "elliptical" poetry, Flarf is accessible and "fun." Roberts writes:

> A flarf poem might use a Google search (say, "Kitty" + "Pizza") and collage the results to form a poem; a flarf poem isn't afraid (mimicking our other popular and news media) to go to the lowest common denominator (see Sharon Mesmer's "Annoying Diabetic Bitch," "Jake Gyllenhall's dog"); a flarf poem rejects over-seriousness!, tossing out tired notions of epiphany (poem-as-discloser-of-elevated-wisdom) and New-Critical (or Poundian) "formal tightness." These aren't poems in search of greatness; in flarfist terms: these poems suck!

While Roberts correctly identifies the importance of "accessibility," he wrongly argues that it can be created by technology and an aesthetic gimmick. Thus, he fails to see how Flarf poets merely repeat the error of the Language poets in superimposing an arbitrary form.

While Flarf poets often understand themselves to be breaking poetic rules, they are simply rejecting some in favor of others. No verse is "free," as Eliot rightly recognized—it is always constrained, even if it is the constraint of not using end-rhyme and meter. Rod Smith makes the ideological constraints of Flarf clear in a recent *Poets and Writers* article: "Aesthetic judgments," he states "about what's bad in a very hierarchal society are usually serving upper-class people with a certain amount of privilege." Thus, Flarf poets write bad poems to challenge such hierarchies. Flarf, it turns out, is of a piece with "elliptical" poetry in this respect. What is needed instead is a return to the natural constraint of complex form. Form makes a poem accessible in terms of its subject matter without which there can be no perception, recognition, or emotional attachment.

In his excellent essay, "The Shape of Poetry," which was first published in AWP's *The Writer's Chronicle* in 1996, Paul Lake argues that sound, meter, and typography are natural to the medium of poetry, and, when used by the poet, function to order the poem. Drawing on chaos theory, Lake argues that a poem is a "strange attractor"—"a high-order, emergent phenomenon" that is formed when it comes into contact with "a simple set of rules." Rhyme and meter are two such rules in poetry. They function as "feedback" devices. They are produced by the phonemes of the poem that, in turn, shape those same phonemes as the poet reads the poem back to himself, cutting a word here, extending a line there.

A third rule, Lake argues, is self-similarity and fractal scaling. Citing Frederick Turner, Lake notes that "the most remarkable use of self-similarity in all of literature" is found in Dante's use of the three line stanza in *The Divine Comedy*, which is "echoed in the Trinitarian theology of its middle-level organization and in the tripartite structure of the whole poem." Self-similarity and fractal scaling are things, Lake argues, that poetry shares with other complex forms in nature, such as the human circulatory system and identical paisley patterns.

Yet, while Lake is right about the naturalness of rule-governed, complex systems such as poems, he wrongly argues, in my view, that such rules derive organically from content alone. Content—no matter how simple—is a constituent of form. It follows, therefore, that content cannot, in the first instance at least, produce the very rules that shape it. Those rules must be, to some degree, independent of content, even if they are, in turn, reflected or reproduced everywhere in it.

Flarf and Form

Lake provides an analogy of how rules determine form at the beginning of the essay that illustrates this very problem. He refers to how Craig Reynolds simulated the flocking behavior of birds by introducing a few simple rules to a number of "autonomous, bird-like agents," as recounted by M. Mitchell Waldrop in his well-known *Complexity: The Emerging Science at the Edge of Order and Chaos*. Of course, a flock was formed, seemingly organically. Yet, it seems to me, it was not formed organically. The rules did not sprout from the "autonomous, bird-like agents" in the program. Reynolds himself introduced a few simple rules, which, in turn, shaped a flock in response to those rules. In fact, Reynolds' experiment, if anything, proved the need for an external, rule-making agent for "form" to be created.

While not without its own problems, Jacques Maritain's work is helpful here. In *Art and Scholasticism*, Maritain notes that the proper end of all art is the perfection of the artifact. This, of course, does not mean that art has no didactic value—far from it. It simply means that art's first commitment is always the formal perfection of the statue, painting, or poem being created.

Unlike Lake, Maritain argues that the rules of art and of poetry exist independent of their respective mediums, even if they are inextricably intertwined with them. These rules are the very rules of God, reflected in the material world and existing independently of matter only in God himself. Rather than "usurping" the rules of God found in nature and superimposing his own rules on form (like Language poets), the true poet, according to Maritain, studies his art to discover the rules present in the material, which, in turn, mirror the rules of his own mind. This is the distinction between the Marxist practice of method and habitus.

Furthermore, while Maritain compares arts such as medicine that "apply themselves to their matter in order to serve it, and to help it to attain a form or a perfection which can be acquired only through the activity of an interior principle" to the fine arts, he goes on to note that because the "interior principle" discovered in the medium of art is "the beautiful," the rules, or variations of rules, are far greater—perhaps even infinite—than the rules discovered for the healing of the body. The beautiful for Maritain did not simply refer to the aural and visual beauty of symmetry and proportion, but there is an intellectual property to beauty as well—clarity and radiance. Thus, seemingly distorted works can also possess a certain beauty, even if many distorted works do not express clarity or radiance, but are intended to merely debunk the notion of order or beauty itself.

Maritain also provides a helpful explanation of why the fine arts, unlike other arts (such as carpentry), are in need of constant renewal. Once "a new adaptation of the fundamental and perennial rules" of art and poetry are applied mechanically to the medium via "pure technique," "the rules formerly living and spiritual become materialized," and a "renewal," a new discovery, "will be necessary." Note that these forms are neither arbitrary (à la Apollinaire) nor political (à la Breton) but "adaptations" of "fundamental," that is pre-existing, rules. Nor do the new forms destroy the old ones. Old forms may become "materialized"—which is to say ubiquitous and, therefore, less capable of re-animating our view of ourselves and the world—but this does not mean that they should be discarded. They should instead by "renewed."

Without rules, there is no order and, therefore, no recognition. And it is recognition that art is all about. Through art, we come face to face, as if for the first time, with the paradoxes of our present existence, or our fractured selves, our yearning for coherence and transcendence, and the beauty and brokenness of creation.

Far from a nostalgic desire to simply return to established forms, what we need is a recognition of the inescapability of form and its roots in the natural order of things. As Rudolf Arnheim argued in his classic study, *Entropy and Art*, absolute formlessness, chaos, is imperceptible. Even seemingly formless things have a form of some sort, however complex. An acceptance of the inescapability of order and the pleasure that its recognition produces in works of art—both paintings and poems—would free poets from the tyranny of a hand-me-down avant-garde that sees art as either a game or a tool in subversion.

Which forms are "natural," one might ask, and what is the criterion of naturalness? In some respects, asking this is like asking a chemist what new isotope he will discover next. Who knows? But when he sees it—as when an astute readers sees life in the rhythms, characters, and voice of a poem—he knows he is onto something worthwhile.

26

A Short History of Form

THE STORY GOES SOMETHING like this: From Chaucer to Wordsworth, English poetry was marked by formal innovation. Shakespeare's sonnets, Donne's epigrams, Milton's line, and Wordsworth's lyrics were indebted to classical Greek and Roman, Anglo-Saxon, and Italian forms, altered by the poets who were guided by excellent literary judgment alone. This formal innovation ceased with the Victorians. Concerned with protecting Protestant morals and establishing an English national identity requisite for a continuing imperialism, the Victorians prescribed certain meters and forms as inherently "Christian" or "natural." George Saintsbury's statement that

> the "iamb, trochee, and anapest" are the "English aristocracy of poetry" (with the iamb, of course, reigning supreme) epitomizes the period's prudery. It is from such arbitrary rules, and the lifeless poetry it created, that avant-garde poets broke free. As Ezra Pound puts it in his Canto 81, *to break the pentameter, that was the first heave.*

This, to use a bit of Anglo-Saxon, is a bunch of crock. While the Victorians did see a clear link between poetic form and religious practice, between meter and national identity, this view, as Kirstie Blair (in *Form and Faith in Victorian Poetry and Religion*) and Meredith Martin (in *The Rise and Fall of Meter*) show, encouraged rather than stifled formal experimentation. The Brownings' interest in "dynamic" form, Edwin Guest's and Walter William Skeat's theories of Anglo-Saxon accent, Gerard Manley Hopkins's "sprung" rhythm, and Robert Bridges's "Britannic foot" were all opposed, in one way or another, to Saintsbury's coining of iambic pentameter as "the English foot." In fact, it is highly unlikely that the free verse of Yeats, Eliot, and Pound would have developed in the way that it did had it not been for the ideas and innovations of the Victorians. Pound's characterization of formal poetry as lifeless and repressive allowed him to define his own work in opposition to it; but the story of English meter at the turn of the century is decidedly more complex than Pound, and many contemporary poets and critics, allowed.

Blair begins with the Tractarians. Evangelical and dissenting poets, such as John Kenyon and Robert and Elizabeth Browning, viewed a strict adherence to religious forms and, by analogy, poetic forms as "restrictive and unnatural, constraining and eventually killing the religious spirit and its hopes for saving grace." High church Tractarians, however, viewed them in exactly the opposite way. For poets like John Keble and Frederick Faber, religious and poetic forms provided the boundaries necessary for life and meaning, mirroring the forms of Christ's church and creation, effectively "channeling" our chaotic passions. In "To the Rothay," for example, Faber addresses the stream, asking it to teach him, by its example of controlled power, to master his own passions through the duty of religious service. This constriction, it turns out, is a blessing, providing both the poet and the poem with "rest": *And by duty narrowed now, / Straight unto that rest I flow*, writes Faber. The poem shows, Blair suggests, "that imposed discipline, in the shape of a channeled stream, may be destructive to the free play of poetic and religious emotion, but is more likely to lead to ultimate salvation through duty and obedience." This differs little in theory from William Carlos Williams's statement that "verse cannot be free in the sense of having no limitations or guiding principles." The question is: Which forms, which rules? And this question, it turns out, was just as open for the Victorians as it was for the moderns.

If Faber's poems were more restrictive than those of most modernists, this does not mean they exhibited no formal experimentation. In his sonnet "The Humiliation," Blair notes, Faber eschews both the Petrarchan and Shakespearean rhyme scheme for one that is impossible to classify, and the final line contains an extra foot. So experimental were "The Humiliation" and Faber's other sonnets that they were lamented by the *Christian Remembrancer* as showing no awareness "of any rule at all, save that of being hedged in by the limits for fourteen lines." And few poets were as experimental as the great Roman Catholic poet Gerard Manley Hopkins.

Hopkins rejected Saintsbury's hybrid model of measuring meter by both syllables (such as in Latin) and accents (such as in Anglo-Saxon). Instead, he believed poets should use stress alone to determine a line of poetry. Relying on stress to structure a poem, Hopkins acknowledged in a letter to Coventry Patmore, would result in "looser" forms.

Yet, as Blair writes, Hopkins's "metrical experimentation was not a signifier of unorthodoxy, but rather . . . a signal of the greater freedom offered by the stricter orthodoxies of Roman Catholicism." Meredith Martin notes that Hopkins's interest in an accentual rather than syllabic meter was related to his idea of how poetry names the "inscape" of things, how it "fetches out" the being of the object named in the poem, as he put it in a piece on Duns Scotus. While Hopkins is often claimed as a proto-modernist, his "metrical experimentations," Martin remarks, "were not ahead of his time; on the contrary, they place him firmly amid the Victorian concerns about the standards and character of the English language." The difference between the Victorians and modernists (such as Pound and Williams) is the view of experimentation as an inherent aspect of orthodoxy and tradition, rather than a rejection of it.

Robert Bridges, one of the Victorian period's most active theorizers of poetic form, is now largely forgotten. But Bridges occupied a sort of third way between the accentual meter of Hopkins (and Skeat and Guest) and the hybrid model of Saintsbury. Bridges argued that either accents or syllables could govern the English line, but not both at the same time. In Milton's *Paradise Lost*, he discovered an alternative to Saintsbury's iambic pentameter in Milton's hexameter, and instead of Saintsbury's "English foot," he proposed a "Britannic foot"—a trisyllabic, mid-stressed foot (exemplified in the name) that he claimed was the commonest example of "stressed verse" in English.

Martin points out that Pound's own ideas regarding English prosody are strikingly similar to those of Bridges. Pound's remark in "A Retrospect" that poets should "compose in the sequence of the musical phrase, not in sequence of a metronome" is suggested with much more nuance in Bridges's "A Letter to a Musician on English Prosody," which was published nearly a decade earlier. Furthermore, Pound's remark "that some poems may have form as a tree has form, some as water poured into a vase" is not unlike Bridges's distinction between accentual and quantitative meter. Martin writes:

> Pound's language supports the narrative of a violent break with the past ... and yet his assumption that any and all metrical systems are hegemonic and rigid belies his ignorance of nineteenth- and early twentieth-century poetics.

As both Blair and Meredith show, the Victorians debated and experimented with poetic form because of its perceived importance both for religious belief and in nourishing a sense of nationhood. It is hard to imagine poetry occupying such a central place in religious and political debates today—marginalized, to put it bluntly, as it has been by a century of avant-garde and so-called post-avant poets who view poetry as a means of attacking, rather than nourishing, the reading public's sensibilities, and form as an oppressive constraint or a mere expression of the poet's personality. This is not to say that there have been no great poets after Pound or Eliot. Yet the simplistic rejection of poetic form after Pound has made it far easier for myriad untalented ideologues to publish work that makes all the right stylistic "moves" but is of little lasting value.

Thankfully, a renewed interest in form is gaining momentum. The *New Criterion*'s poetry prize, the *Contemporary Poetry Review*, two new writing programs that emphasize the craft of form, and an increasing number of talented "formal" poets all point to this growing interest in poetic form. Here, however, the myth of stable English verse-forms, rejected by dissipated bohemians and now in need of recovery, is an equally tempting but false narrative. No doubt a closer attention to patterned language, to sound, to the freedom of control, is in need of recovery. This recovery, however, should continue, not merely replicate, the formal successes of the past.

27

Is Free Verse Immoral?

Is it "incongruous" or immoral, as Mark Signorelli argues in an intriguing pair of essays at *Public Discourse*, to write or read free verse? I don't think so, but let me start with what I think Signorelli gets right.

In the first essay, Signorelli argues that the free verse and fragmentation found in modern poetry embody a "debased" yearning for an individual freedom "severed from all obligation to tradition, nature, or rationality." Free verse expresses the dream of an individual will free of the "essential ends" of the art of poetry, even if this means the death of poetry. In the case of fragmentation, it is the dream of an individual will free from rational coherence, even if, ironically, this means the death of the subject. "That is why," Signorelli states, it is incongruous, and perhaps even immoral, for poets to fill "journals with free-verse modernist-style creations." In the second essay, he argues that poets must return to the "essential ends" of the art—teaching and delighting.

I think Signorelli hits a number of right notes. First, there is no question that all forms of art and poetry embody "some identifiable ethical or cosmological perspective," though, as I will argue shortly, they cannot easily be reduced to one perspective. Second, Signorelli is right that free verse is rooted *in part* in a longing for autonomy. Third, I share what I sense to be Signorelli's frustration with what passes for poetry today. Many poems lack craft and intellectual rigor, and turn to shock value or the political screed to garner some attention. I agree that the use of meter and rhyme would do much to reinvigorate contemporary poetry. Fourth, I share Signorelli's concern for a lack of thoughtful engagement with both poetry and the arts. Too often we reject unthinkingly or love indiscriminately.

Signorelli's argument rests on the premise that all artifacts embody the spirit of the age in which they are produced. The spirit of the modern age is relativism; therefore, Signorelli concludes, free verse can be rightly understood as embodying this relativism. Although this is true to an extent, it is overly reductive. Works of art—particularly great ones—embody, yes, but also transcend their ages. This is what makes them great. They are not *merely* reflective of the ideas or preoccupations of a certain people from a certain time in a certain place, but of the unchanging human heart as well. This is why people from other times and other places find them compelling. If the ideas of a particular age are particularly bad, this makes transcendence more difficult, but not impossible.

While we can lament the poverty of our modern age and attest, as Signorelli does, that the art of our age expresses this poverty, it is an error to reject particular formal inventions *on the evidence of this rational link alone*. The question is, then, does free verse *only* embody this "decadent" yearning for a personal freedom "severed from all obligation to tradition, nature, or rationality"? And if not, is what it does embody or allow to be expressed of any value?

I would argue that poets turned to free verse (or a precursor of free verse) for other reasons than a simple longing for individual freedom. Wordsworth's attempt to use a selection of "common" diction in *Lyrical Ballads* and *The Prelude* is clearly a precursor of free verse. Reacting against Alexander Pope's claim for a universal diction present in neo-classical poetry, Wordsworth incorporated elements of low diction in an effort to provide a more accurate representation of human nature. There is a higher and lower element to man, Wordsworth argued. We are both ethereal and earthy. And so he turned to lower diction, among other reasons, to balance what he understood to be the *untruth* of an overly stylized, ornate diction that ignored man's fleshly nature and common diction.

We find a similar motive, surprisingly enough, in French surrealism. While there is a fair share of yearning for a "debased" autonomy in surrealism, the use of fractured syntax and absurd images was also motivated by a rejection of nineteenth-century positivism that tacitly reduced man to pure rationality—a point Marcel Raymond makes in his classic study *De Baudelaire au surréalisme*. Breton co-opted this for his own ideological ends, but it is nevertheless true that the *partial* goal of both Wordsworth's diction and the surrealists' free verse fragments is a more accurate representation of human experience as it is actually lived.

Is Free Verse Immoral?

An example of the value of a good free verse poem is helpful here. Yves Bonnefoy's first book of poems was published in 1953. He was originally associated with the surrealists, but broke with Breton when he refused to sign "Rupture inaugurale." While his earliest poems are marked by a certain ideological "militantism," his work has been almost universally lauded since that first volume. This poem is entitled "A Bit of Water":

> I long to grant eternity
> To this flake
> That alights on my hand,
> By making my life, my warmth,
> My past, my present days
> Into a moment: the boundless
> Moment of now
> But already it's no more
> Than a bit of water, lost in the fog
> Of bodies moving through snow.

I have chosen this poem because, on the surface, it seems to illustrate Signorelli's thesis. Here the poet longs "to grant eternity" to the snowflake on his hand by making it the subject of a poem. Bonnefoy, who is an indefatigable translator of Shakespeare, is no doubt alluding to Shakespeare's Sonnet 18 (and the many classical precedents) in which he proposes to grant his subject life after death in his "eternal lines." In writing about the snowflake, however, the poet also hopes to grant himself eternity. After all, the snowflake is observed from his perspective. Thus, something of his own life attaches itself to the snowflake—which is wonderfully illustrated in the flake alighting on the poet's hand—and passes with the snowflake in the poem into a "boundless / Moment of now." The free verse embodies, as Signorelli would say, this longing for a boundless present, and the enjambment in line six and seven neatly captures this longing for boundlessness.

But here's the rub: the snowflake melts before the poet can grant it and himself eternity. It has become "no more / Than a bit of water," which, ironically, becomes the title of the poem. Here we have an acknowledgment that poetry—even free verse poetry—cannot save the flake from melting or the poet from the constraints of finitude. This is a fact that Shakespeare only acknowledges grudgingly in Sonnet 18. In the end, this is not a poem that misleads us into believing that we are autonomous individuals free from all constraints. Rather, it shows how we all long for such freedom, and how we can never possess it through our own power. The tension between the free verse and the repetition and closure (as well as the dichotomy of past and present, snow and "warmth") of this poem expresses this twofold truth of human existence. Nor does this poem end in relativism, but in agnosticism. The poet knows these two things, but he leaves the question of what we are to do in light of them unanswered.

Does the structure of this poem embody a depraved desire to free the self from all constraints? Does it express an epistemological relativism? Is it marked by a paucity of truth? Is it an attack on the reader's sensibilities and the "essential elements" of poetry? Is it marked by "a perfect indifference toward the *telos* of his art"? In other words, does it fail to teach and please?

The answer to all of these questions, I think, is no. In fact, one could even argue that his poem is distinctly "incarnational," embodying the meaning of the particular piece (the desire for an eternal present coupled with the recognition that such an eternal present cannot be brought about through poetry) in the flesh of the form.

All poetry is constrained in some way or another, and almost all so-called "modernist" poets recognized this. In 1942, T. S. Eliot stated famously that "No verse is free for the man who wants to do a good job." William Carlos Williams wrote that "Being an art form, verse cannot be free in the sense of having no limitations or guiding principles." Williams himself experimented with what he called a "triadic line." Even the staunchest of anti-formalists, the $L=A=N=G=U=A=G=E$ poets, cannot shake all formal constraints, as Paul Lake has shown in his essay "The Enchanted Loom." Internal rhymes, repetition, syntactic hierarchies, self-similarity, fractal scaling, and so forth assert themselves again and again.

Bonnefoy's poem, for example, is full of self-similarity, repetition, and syntactic hierarchies, and it is helpful to briefly consider these items in original French, which don't come through as clearly in the translation. The first part of the poem uses the repetition of "de," which can be translated as "of" or "to" in English, to highlight the speaker's "desire" in the poem *to* grant eternity, *to* transform his life, *to* transform his past, *into* a single, eternal moment. The word appears five times in three lines in parallel structure, reinforcing the poet's strong wish that he could by human agency (hence the "to") do this one thing. The first stanza ends with the phrase "sans bornes" or "without bounds," once again mirroring the speaker's desire to escape all constraint (perhaps even the constraint of art) in this final phrase that dangles temptingly at the end. The final lines repeat the phoneme [s] seven times, which could be read as imitating the sound of a snake. Is this Satan speaking, promising a life like God—an eternal present without limits? This fantasy (or temptation), however, is answered with the first word of the second and final stanza: "Mais" or "But." The snowflake has melted and has become nothing more than a "peu d'eau," lost in the fog and "bodies" moving through the snow. The reality of death, in other words, puts paid to the speaker's dream (and Satan's lie), and I don't think it is by chance that the second stanza is half the length of the opening stanza's six lines.

In the end, Signorelli's hasty rejection of free verse and idealization of traditional poetic forms not only fails to take into account the formal pleasures of free verse, it also oversimplifies how poetic forms develop and work. All forms are invented. Chaucer's heroic couplet, Dante's *terza rima*, Petrarch's sonnet did not fall from the sky. They were created as these poets explored human experience in language, informed by their respective understandings of who we are and what there is. The development of traditional forms and free verse in English, as H. T. Kirby Smith has pointed out in *The Origins of Free Verse*, is much messier than is often acknowledged, by "organicists" and formalists alike.

Furthermore, in simply returning to traditional forms—which is what Signorelli seems to have in mind when he calls us to return to "formally structured, consecutively ordered verse"—without exploring current human experience in language, the poet runs the risk of becoming a grammarian, skilled in the technique of poetic forms but lacking in virtuous insight.

I, too, believe that contemporary poetry can be reinvigorated by an incorporation of meter and rhyme, but rather than simply rejecting free verse as immoral, a better solution would be for poets to open themselves up to the possibility of rhyme and meter, using it when appropriate as they explore language in search of *new* forms that communicate the truth of who we are and what there is to living individuals. After all, art is a communal act, and the artist must write poems that meet his own satisfaction but also serve his audience.

28

An Avant-Garde Presbyterian

IT IS NOT UNCOMMON for so-called avant-garde poets to complain that no one reads poetry anymore and to blame capitalism for the lack of interest. Capitalism, it is argued, has "commodified" language, thus "alienating" us from ourselves and from others. We think of ourselves in clichés that have been created by the market and act out those clichés by buying all sorts of stuff, except poetry.

And why not poetry? Because poetry—the *real* stuff, not the fun, comforting verse of Billy Collins—subverts commodified language. It shows us that we are not football-loving men, fathers, husbands, good Christians, loyal middle-managers, and so forth—that the market has hoodwinked us into using these terms to sell stuff, but that these words do not express who we are. Poetry shakes us, and we don't want to be shaken. We don't want to know that we've lived a lie, that even the idea of the self is a lie, and that we only have meaning to the extent that we live in egalitarian communion with others and nature. Poetry is "violent" because capitalism is "violent."

Aaron Belz is a different sort of avant-garde poet. He studied under Allen Ginsberg and Philip Levine, but he is also a Presbyterian (his family is associated with *World Magazine* and Covenant College), a father of three, entrepreneur, and former small business owner. While we have, of course, deluded ourselves with all sorts of lies—greed and the philosophical materialism of Marxism included—Belz refrains from self-righteously attacking the "bourgeois" or "subverting" in some pretentious way the lies we tell ourselves. His tools are satire and self-deprecating humor. His third collection of poetry, *Glitter Bomb*, is an anti-self-help book wrapped in shimmering plastic. It's alternatingly fun and serious, sad and playful, lonely and hopeful. In fact, it's a deeply Christian book without ever mentioning Christ by name.

Belz is a master of the poetic deadpan. "There is no I in team," he writes in "Team," "but there's one in bitterness / and one in failure." And in "Interesting About You," he writes: "What's interesting about you / Is the unique ways in which / You fail to distinguish yourself."

Epigrams are traditionally two- to four-line poems that often offer witty conundrums. John Donne's epigrams, for example, rely on classical allusions and logic games. Belz's epigrams, like the two above, at first seem all surface but end up telling us something about ourselves—in this case, that we are bitter failures, that we have very little interest in "taking one for the team," despite the value-heavy rhetoric of contemporary youth sports, that we are all preoccupied with ourselves above all else.

Many of his other poems work the same way. Take "One Star," for example, which also begins with wordplay. "Of star-crossed lovers and cross-eyed lovers," Belz writes, "fate favors the latter; at least they are together." The distinction between "star-crossed" and "cross-eyed" seems merely funny at first. But with one phrase ("at least they are together"), which initially seems campy (Is he referring to the cross-eyed lovers' *eyes* being closer together?), Belz manages to say something true—that love is about *being together* more so than passion—without sounding self-consciously wise. He is, in this sense, the anti-Khalil Gibran.

Belz is indebted to Frank O'Hara, but unlike Ted Berrigan, who aped O'Hara's style with little interest in O'Hara's larger questions, Belz's poetry reminds us of the way we use language to hide our loneliness or construct some meaning out of the disparate moments of our lives. In "Accumulata," Belz asks:

> So you string together a number of moments
> and you call it *life*? You say *My life*?
> And is there a moment in which you notice
> this moment is disconnected from the rest?

"And this / being the case," he continues, "do you not regard the darker drops":

> the desperate drops, the drops of horror,
> drops of failure, flat drops, mingled or rather
> inexplicably interleaved with the funny,

> the sunshiny, the naps, and see, can't you see
> that this is your ordinary? That these, each
> and each, and all, are neither total nor definitive
> but are rather, say, *She left*. There is a
> moment for it. Or *The last words she spoke*,
> which haunts you like a bell whose peal
> continues to echo down dreams.
> That these, none of them, will damn you.

Here Belz is riffing on the post-structuralist insight (one seconded by Walker Percy) that we cannot construct a narrative that makes sense of ourselves. We always leave something out. Yet, we construct them nonetheless in a failed effort to save ourselves, to give ourselves a name or a meaning that ignores our failures, and even the many bittersweet, mingled moments of life. We don't want to be damned by our failures, and so we write them out of our life, instead of recognizing that these moments can't damn us if we turn to Christ.

This all makes *Glitter Bomb* sound overly serious. It's not, or, it is serious while having a lot of fun. We have poems like "Avatar" in which Belz writes:

> Blue computer graphics woman
> with smooth cat nose, you are
> purer, more in touch with nature,
> and actually quite a bit taller than I—
> and although you've discovered
> that your soul mate is really just a
> small, physically challenged white guy
> gasping for air in a mobile home,
> you've decided to stick with him.
> I'd taken you for one of those shallow
> pantheistic utopian cartoon giantesses,
> but now I see that I was way off.

Or "Tuberculosis Day," where Belz writes: "The acronym / we're going to use / for Tuberculosis Day / is TBD." But Belz is too honest to let us off the hook for long. Life is full of failures. We are, Belz writes,

An Avant-Garde Presbyterian

a kind of ever-setting sun—your
own life's most familiar error,
repeated in the company of those
you'd hoped would love you most.

This is not dishonest bleakness, but an acknowledgement of our profound fallenness, and of the inability of any language—the language of capitalism, Marxism, or poetry—to save us.

29

Orpheus in the Bronx

REGINALD SHEPHERD WAS ONE of those rare figures whose difficult childhood, which should have thwarted any great accomplishment, spurred him on to exactly that. Born in 1963 and raised mostly in the Bronx by his single mother, Shepherd oscillated between inner-city public schools and, funded by scholarships and government support, private, posh day schools. Ostracized at the former for being smart and at the latter for being "poor and black," his early experience of the world was one of estrangement. "Even when I found someone whom I thought actually understood me," Shepherd would later write, "I would always eventually come up against a wall between us." This sense of being lost in a world in which he did not belong was compounded by his mother's early death. She was his sole attachment to the physical world beside books, and when she died, Shepherd would later write, "the world ended." He was fifteen at the time.

Enamored with poetry since the ninth grade after reading T. S. Eliot's "The Love Song of J. Alfred Prufrock," Shepherd would eventually complete an undergraduate degree at Bennington College and two MFAs—one at Brown and another at Iowa. He went on to write five collections of poems before he died of cancer in 2008.

His work was first recognized by Carolyn Forché, winning the Association of Writers and Writing Programs' Award in Poetry in 1993. Dense, complex, playful, and steeped in Western mythology, this first selection of poems, *Some Are Drowning*, would also win the "Discovery"/*The Nation* award, announcing Shepherd as a major poetic talent. His next volume of poems was *Angel, Interrupted* in 1996, followed by *Wrong* (1999), *Otherhood* (2003), and *Fata Morgana* (2007).

In these volumes, Shepherd attempts to transform his overwhelming sense of alienation into temporary reconciliation by creating a "mythology" of himself and his relation to the world. In the opening sequence of poems in *Fata Morgana*, he is Orpheus to his mother's Calliope. His stunted interest in astronomy regains a central space in his poems, and moments of loss or suffering—the squalor of the Bronx apartment, missing maternal and paternal affection, nightmares—are redeemed in his work by virtue of their inclusion in something beautiful: the poem itself.

This effort to transform his broken life through art continues in the posthumous collection, *Red Clay Weather*. Addressing both the reader and himself, he writes in "Along with Whatever Has Not Yet Been Named": "Take if you will this improbable boy":

> Take if you will this boy made out
> of wish and will-not-ever-be, made out
> to be something he's not, breeze
> through the trees. Puzzle his riddling
> skin, his irrigated desert
> body couched in eroding
> mountains. Ride out the rustling sibilants
> and make a man into an effigy:
> of summer skin, the last exemplar.

This transformed "summer skin," this "effigy," is the beautiful myth of the poet's identity and his belonging in a world that is part of himself. Poetry begins "in the midst of things / that split or burn or tear the skin," Shepherd writes in "Days Like Survival," transforming "this elegant, unkempt earth / of rust and dust, smashed cat and armadillo / roadkill," into a Baudelarian "fine scum."

Water, one of Shepherd's favorite symbols, is a recurring image in *Red Clay Weather*. Like poetry, it is both a destructive and constructive force, eroding and shaping the landscape—in Shepherd's words, "framing" the raw "facts" of the material world. "Air's violent / poetry," Shepherd writes in "Seize the Day," "is saturated with salvation / and heavy rains, silt fills the mouth / instead of words, settling into red clay gullies / erosion scrawls down mobile / slopes."

And water's reflection, like art's, can both awaken us to the beauty of our surroundings and tempt us into Narcissistic self-absorption. As Shepherd writes in "Narcissus Before the Rain," "The carriers of water bring their own / extinction. He tried to think his way through / himself, there wasn't any person deep enough." Water cleanses, shapes, and destroys.

Shepherd's view of poetry as mythology, like Wallace Stevens's, suffers from a theoretical problem both Stevens and Shepherd recognized. For Stevens, while poetry is the "supreme fiction," it is also always inorganic, lifeless. This is the lesson of "Anecdote of the Jar," where the poet places a jar—the primordial artifact—on a hill in Tennessee, providing order to the otherwise "slovenly wilderness," which rises up to it "no longer wild." Yet, while the jar takes "dominion" of the wilderness, the rub is that it does not "give of bird or bush, / Like nothing else in Tennessee."

Shepherd identifies this same problem in his essay "Why I Write": "I have a strong sense of the fragility of the things we shore up against the ruin which is life: the fragility of natural beauty but also the artistic beauty, which is meant to arrest death but embodies death in that very arrest." This is the "aporia of art."

How to avoid this impasse? This is the second preoccupation of *Red Clay Weather*. One could make the case that art's ability to "redeem" alienation reflects Christ's actual redemption of the world. In Dostoevsky's *The Idiot*, the naïve, innocent Prince Myshkin states famously that beauty will "save the world." While the phrase is somewhat enigmatic, the beauty to which Myshkin refers is neither the human beauty of Aglaya nor the man-made beauty of art but rather the divine beauty of Christ. Christ endured "infinite suffering" to transform the chaos of our sin in his death *and* resurrection into ordered righteousness. And unlike beautiful art—which, in Shepherd's words, always "kills,"—Christ is risen.

In "God-With-Us," the final poem of *Red Clay Weather*, Shepherd compares Christ, whose birth is announced by a star, with the mythologies of the Greco-Roman gods, whose own stars populate Shepherd's poems:

> What will I call you
> when you are gone?
> How will I know your name?
> Little star, reflection
> on the Sea of Galilee,
> a lantern in the wood, half-hid,
> half-seen?

reflecting on what can't be
touched, be known?

***

star of milk, star of a
nursing child's mouth, my
child, my lord, whoever
you may be today, tonight
which will not end, a cup
passed to me, from which I may
or may not drink, half-empty
star, still asleep by now?
And your small body, Emmanuel,
(how small my heart
to fit inside yours)
lies there, pearled, asleep . . .
How I want to believe.
(a pearl, an irritant).

Of his early attraction to mythology, Shepherd wrote: "Those myths' world of power and beauty and force corresponded much more to my sense of the world ruled by arbitrary powers answerable to no one than did the ethical prescriptions of Christianity, whose threats were always more believable than its promises, and whose insistence on a world ruled by law and justice and a moral order bore no resemblance to the world I suffered every day." Yet in this poem that concludes his last book, the cold power of mythology's gods is contrasted with the humble power of grace. Here we have a God who descends to man, becoming a weak, suckling child, in order to save. This God is indeed different from the cruel, misanthropic Greco-Roman gods of pure force. In this final poem, Shepherd captures the essence of what makes the "star" of Christianity unlike the mythical "stars" of the Greco-Romans. And it is something that both attracts and repels Shepherd. It is "a pearl, an irritant."

Robert Philen informs us in his introduction to the volume that Shepherd wrote this poem "in late August 2008 from his hospital bed, about two weeks before his death." It was around this time that Shepherd was also baptized into the Episcopal Church. It is difficult not to lament the poems he might have written following this conversion, if it indeed was a true turning. What insights might the language of faith have opened up for a poet with Shepherd's sensibilities? Yet, what he left us are hard, gem-like poems of a precocious, God-haunted boy from the Bronx—a beautiful gift, nonetheless.

30

Life's Duplicity

THE FIRST POEM OF Devin Johnston's penultimate collection, *Far-Fetched*, is a ruse. The poet addresses Sally Hen, asking her, "how do you like your home?" He describes the chicken coop ("A straight run from east to west / with hardscrabble fit for a choral dance") and Sally herself in simple, fluid prose, heightened by only a few striking metaphors that are nevertheless entirely natural ("you softly cluck, then settle down / to roost in mercury-vapor light / with spring behind your lids."). Sally bends "on backward knees / to crop a tussock of cloverleaf." She notices the "snowmelt" and the "breath of wind." Spring will soon take hold. The scene is nearly idyllic.

Like all good narrative poems, however, there's a turn in the final lines, though not in what happens (Sally laying an egg, which is entirely predictable) but in how Johnston describes it:

> From a fallow bed, so much undone,
> your parched and reptilian cry proclaims
> a perfect form of incompletion:
> first egg of the year.

The phrase "perfect form of incompletion" is a wonderful description of an egg as an egg, but it's more than that. We see that spring itself is also a "perfect form of incompletion," being but a temporary respite from the "lord of ice" walnut tree above the coop. The hen's "parched and reptilian cry" that "proclaims" the egg is the cry of survival, perhaps, or one that announces that the upcoming spring does not offer freedom but another kind of lordship—the demands of instinct or passion that can never be satisfied, leaving "so much undone" or always more to do. Spring may be a metaphor for life, but it is also a reminder that we too "bend on backward knees," broken by appetite.

It is also a poem about America. The title is "Ameraucana," and the coop is evocative of how we sometimes think of the States—"A straight run from the east to the west." Read as such, the poem points to our failure to be that voice crying out in the wilderness, as some Colonialists had hoped, to "make straight in the desert a highway for our God," to quote Isaiah.

As he does here, Johnston makes the most of poetry's duplicity—its ability to express the doubleness of life—throughout the volume. We are evil and noble at the same time, foolish and wise, incurably selfish yet capable of great acts of kindness. Life is funny and pathetic. Nature both renews our spirits and reminds us that death is inescapable. He feels no need to choose between seemingly contradictory truths, no need "to say it all," and so often says more.

In "New Song," for example, which is based on a poem by the medieval troubadour Guillaume IX, Duke of Aquitaine, the speaker recounts the "thorny hawthorn spray" of young love and advances spurned by a young woman until "one April morning" she relents, "relented without warning, / relenting from her cold rebuff / in laughter, peals of happiness." The speaker cries out in adolescent pique: "Sweet Christ, let me live long enough / to get my hands beneath her dress!" The final stanza puts the lesson this way:

> I hate the elevated talk
> that disregards both root and stalk
> and sets insipid pride above
> vicissitudes of lust and strife.
> Let others claim a higher love:
> we've got the bread, we've got the knife.

The poem could be read as a straightforward celebration of youth, love, and carnal pleasures over religious or intellectual ones, but the religious imagery allows us to read the couple's experience metaphorically, as an image of the ravishing passion, the silly joy, we should have for "Sweet Christ" himself. Sex does bring us closer to God to the extent that it is a cognate of that higher abandon.

But sex and other desires can also leave us wanting and wounded, as the "knife" in the final line makes all too clear. This is a lesson we learn early, as Johnston shows in "Want," where a parent tells a spouse listening to a crying infant: "Let the child cry awhile / with a rasp that strains his throat. // Let him learn what can't be satisfied / and break him like a colt." Later in the poem, Johnston reminds us of "the hollow tap / of appetite."

In "Turned Loose," we have a refreshingly honest portrait of the paradox of parenthood. On Sunday, a father disregards "the impulse / to be free" of his children who "cling" to him "like burrs" in a crowded museum. On Monday at the office, however, he wants "nothing but their presence, / my ears attuned to outdoors / and the timber of their voices." In "Visiting Day," a poem that reminds me of Vernon Scannell's "jailbird" poem, Johnston uses the flat, prescriptive language governing prison visits to reveal the irony and pain of the event:

> Do not share food or drinks.
> No rubbing arms or touching faces.
> Visitors and offenders may
> hold hands across the table.
> You will only be permitted
> one greeting and departing kiss,
> a closed-mouth kiss
> of one to two seconds.
> Do not leave children unattended

Johnston's range is impressive. The volume contains a number of poems on birds, fish, and sailing, as well as lighter landscape pieces. He switches back and forth between more narrative poems and more "objective" ones, where nouns almost carry the action and sounds ricochet from one image to the next. In "Above Ivanhoe," for example, he writes:

> A colt's tail drags a scruff,
> a handbreadth of cloud
> skiffing across the gap,
> its wake a drow of cold breath,
> a mug of dirty light, tipping out
> reflections from a daguerreotype

In "Late October," a hawk and starling "sport / through all this rigging / of blocks and lines / counterweights and arbors // the street / a theater set for storms." And in "Ting," Johnston describes the song of a bellbird in terms that could almost be applied to his own work: "unchanging yet arrhythmic

/ cool yet intimate," it "gathers fog around it / to sound the hush / and make it sing."

Phrases regularly surprise with their evocativeness and specificity—not an easy combination. In one poem, he refers to the River Clyde as "the idle tracing of a mood / with purposeless exactitude," and in another "sub-aquatic / light renders / ironwork remote." His previous volume, *Traveller* (2011), was praised for its "texture" and "precision," and rightly so. *Far-Fetched* is more personal, it seems to me, and the better for it—a wise and rewarding collection.

31

Ernest Hilbert's Street Music

MOST AMERICANS DON'T LIKE to talk about death, but Ernest Hilbert doesn't mind. Death and decay is what he sees in *Caligulan*—his third volume of poems after *Sixty Sonnets* (2009) and *All of You on the Good Earth* (2013)—and he has little interest in spinning "Fictions fielding hopes of glory / Where none should be fulfilled." This is a question of temperament, as the title suggests, and reality. However we might feel, it's relatively clear that the "seams" of order, as Hilbert puts it in one poem, have been "unsewn."

Caligulan is organized according to the seasons, beginning with "Summer," and immediately something's not right—not so much with summer itself but with how we imagine it. It may be a moment to sip margaritas in Antigua, but it's also an occasion to watch a one-footed seagull poke at the trash on a pier at Barnegat Light, New Jersey:

> The stump's a small sharp spear that stings the bird
> If ground is touched. He soars to foggy scree,
> Alights but flaps to halfway hang in air, spurred
> By pain to perform endless pirouettes.

The seagull's not the only bird in the volume—there are also ospreys, blue jays, and hawks—and like these, the gull is an omen. "Summer," Hilbert writes, "is the center" of the gull's circling and of our lives that "we try to pretend / Will keep us strong, like love, and never end." In reality, it is, at best, a momentary reprieve from life's sting. To expect anything more from it is delusional. "Friends," Hilbert writes in another poem, "tell me I should be *happier*":

> But to think is to appreciate that even
> This sunshine—brilliant, primeval balm—will burn
> If I linger too long, that it can blur
> A universe of details to blindness when
> One stares fixedly . . .

It is to avoid such blindness that Hilbert, metaphorically, avoids staring at the sun in the volume. Instead, he looks at farting ATVs, a castrated horse whose testicles are fed to dogs (in the "Spring" section of the volume—you get the idea), daffodils in sidewalk cracks that are "decorated / By the locust shells of Trojans and Nestle's," and a supermodel who falls on the street while paparazzi take pictures in a semicircle and her boyfriend laughs.

As anti-pastoral as Hilbert can be, he shares Robert Frost's commitment to describing impressions as precisely as possible, which may offer, as it did Frost, a "momentary stay against confusion," even if such descriptions can lead to contradictory conclusions. In one poem, for example, a hawk "seems almost a sign // That nothing kills more than it creates, / Or is wrong with what we finally become." In another, however, Hilbert suggests that we are, or are becoming, monsters. Looking into dark water from the deck of a boat, he asks:

> But where is our monster, the one we thought
> Would always be there somewhere, though hidden?
> The tiny girl in pink stamps her silver slippers.
> No monster today, or ever. I catch the shallow
> Smudges of my face in the cabin window.

Poetry is "real," but it's also a balm for Hilbert. Like the pirouettes of the seagull in the opening poem, poetry soothes us with its rhythm until death brings oblivion. "Your love weeps all night. At dawn, she screams," Hilbert writes in "Kingdom of Spiders":

> You can't know what designs more pain might bring.
> Cold streets fill with crowds. You want to fight.
> You spit and shout. In daydreams you sing.

Here again, then, we have the old paradox of poetry (and perhaps all art) as both a reflection of and an escape from reality encapsulated neatly in a single quatrain.

Hilbert's father was a classically trained musician and teacher who used to play Bach and Rachmaninoff at night or in the morning. Hilbert, who currently works as a rare book dealer in Philadelphia and has a doctorate in English from Oxford, learned the piano as a child and played in a heavy metal band as a teen. The music of *Caligulan* is, by turns, smooth and jagged. This is by design. Poetry reflects and clarifies complexity. Still, some of Hilbert's lines seem unintentionally rough, and there are one or two that are little more than confections. The purpose of one irregular sonnet on flying a kite, for example, seems to be simply to set up the final clever, but mostly empty, paradox: "A thing apart; though still tethered / Fatherless, and finally unfathered."

But overall, the volume is full of skillful surprises and insight, as well as occasional moments of humor. In a poem on a "Zombie Fun Run," Hilbert writes sarcastically: "No point being dull / When waging war on a disease that kills."

An honest volume for dishonest times, *Caligulan* reminds us that "thunder / Sinks your song, because, like the day of birth, / The day you'll wake and have your death is set." It "just hasn't happened yet."

32

The Faithful Poetry of Christian Wiman

ALL POETRY IS COMPARISON. One thing resembles another—a squirrel is an itch, for example—and the poet notes the relation by metaphor, repetition, sound. Sometimes the comparison is stated, sometimes it is implied, and sometimes it is made through characters. Bad poems can be bad for a number of reasons, but banal or inscrutable comparisons are common flaws. In the one case, the comparison is so obvious as to bore; in the other, it makes no sense because it is merely private or mangled by shoddy thinking.

In his first collection of selected poems, *Hammer Is the Prayer*, Christian Wiman, the former editor of *Poetry*, compares things by accumulation. Many of his poems begin in media res, with a response to a question or a thought about a previous event, and progress by observation. Sometimes the speaker addresses a "you," sometimes not. While a handful of poems take on the voice of a character, many are straight lyrics, written in a voice that alternates between description (of an apocalyptic Texas landscape, for example, or downtown Chicago) and intonation ("I am a ghost of all I don't remember, / a grown man standing where a child once stood") with an occasional touch of playfulness.

His style, in other words, or his primary style in the volume, is very much the fashion. But a couple of things set him apart. The first is the precision and clarity of his language. It's easy to throw adjectives and nouns together to create an image that seems evocative (or provocative) but fails to evoke much at all. This is what makes surrealistic poetry both fun and frustrating to read. After the cheap thrill of contrasting images (as in Tristan Tzara's "Vegetable Swallows," which has lines like "the nimble stags storms cloud over / rain falls under the scissors of / the dark hairdresser-furiously / swimming under the clashing arpeggios"), a hunger sets in for something substantial.

Wiman never takes such shortcuts. He risks saying what he means. The "fevered air" and "green delirium" of leaves "whipped and quickened" by a thunderstorm mirror a late relative's "sudden eloquent confusion." One poem opens:

> It is good to sit even a rotting body
> in sunlight uncompromised
> by God, or lack of God,
>
> to see the bee beyond
> all the plundered flowers
> air-stagger toward you

In another, which touches on his experience as a cancer patient that eventually led him back to the Christian faith, he writes:

> Incurable and unbelieving
> in any truth but the truth of grieving,
>
> I saw a tree inside a tree
> rise kaleidoscopically
>
> as if the leaves had livelier ghosts.

In "Keynote," the speaker feels in a dream, "the Sisyphean satisfaction of a landscape / adequate to loss."

Wiman, as the above selections show, also has an excellent ear and turns to various kinds of repetition to mostly great effect. Reversals of structure (chiasmus) and inversion (anastrophe) are used frequently—maybe too frequently—but not heavy handedly. His mix of internal and end rhyme gives his poems a quickness and coherence, and his religious verse, like Donne's, is both immediate and meditative. "When the time's toxins / have seeped into every cell," Wiman writes in one poem,

> somehow a seed
> of belief

> sprouts the instant
> I acknowledge it:
>
> little weedy hardy would-be
> greenness
>
> tugged upward
> by light

There are, unfortunately, a handful of otherwise taut poems that are marred, in my view, by a sudden over-articulation. In a wonderful poem set in Prague, for example, the speaker sees a falcon on a windowsill as a woman walks out of the bath behind him, naked, "dripping, as a bloom // of blood" forms on her cheek:

> Wish for something, you said.
> A shiver pricked your spine.
> The falcon turned its head
> and locked its eyes on mine

What a shame that these beautiful lines are followed by this final stanza:

> and for a long moment I'm still in
> I wished and wished and wished
> the moment would not end.
> And just like that it vanished.

The feeling suddenly seems trumped up. Is he really still "in" the moment—especially if "it" along with the falcon vanished the instant he wished it lasted? The repetition of "wished" communicates a kind of straining, but not the right kind.

In "One Time," his confession that "I do not know how to come closer to God / except by standing where a world is ending / for one man" makes it seem like he's trying too hard to make the important statement, especially when it is followed by "and for an hour I have listened / to the breathing of the woman I love beyond / my ability to love." The use of repetition for mimetic or rhetorical effect falls flat in a few others. A pumpjack bows to the ground "Again, again, again" in one poem. In another, leaves are "Spinning and spinning without sound." "I come back to the world. I come back / to the world," he writes in a poem on the Canyon de Chelly, "and would speak of it plainly, / with only so much artifice as words / themselves require." Alas, not always.

Still, *Hammer Is the Prayer* is full of far more successes than partial successes. The volume also shows Wiman's skill at narrative and translation. He includes the wonderful long poem "Being Serious" (the title alludes to Wilde's *The Importance of Being Earnest*) from *Hard Night*, and a selection of his Osip Mandelstam translations. Few poets today can write lines like this: "I have no illusion / some fusion / of force and form / will save me, / bewilderment / of bonelight / ungrave me."

33

Dana Gioia's Articulation

HE HASN'T WON A Pulitzer—yet—but make no mistake about it: Dana Gioia is one of the best American poets writing today, and his latest volume proves it.

Organized topically ("Mystery," "Place," "Love," to name three of seven) rather than by previously published collections, *99 Poems: New and Selected* is a book for readers, not scholars. Fifteen of the poems are new. The rest have been selected from his previous four collections. All of them show a master at work.

This is a book of seemingly insignificant things—a photograph, a tree, a Beach Boys song, a long dead uncle remembered. Why? Nothing "is hidden in the obvious / changes of the world." Or, as he puts it in "The Stars Now Rearrange Themselves Above You":

> The stars now rearrange themselves above you
> but to no effect. Tonight,
> only for tonight, their powers lapse,
> and you must look toward earth. There will be
> no comets now, no pointing star
> to lead where you know you must go.
>
> Look for smaller signs instead, the fine
> disturbances of ordered things when suddenly
> the rhythms of your expectation break.

That those "disturbances of ordered things" are formally reflected in the poem's enjambment, caesuras, and trochees suggests that poetry is the "microscope" that helps us *see*, to borrow Emily Dickinson's metaphor in "'Faith' Is a Fine Invention," to which "The Stars Now Rearrange Themselves Above You" is, perhaps, a response. Ironically, it is in looking "toward earth" that "another world / reveals itself behind the ordinary."

To say that this world "reveals itself" is to reject the idea that the poet is a priest or a little god who endows the world with a significance not its own. "The world does not need words," Gioia writes, "It articulates itself / in sunlight, leaves, and shadows. The stones on the path / are no less real for lying uncatalogued and uncounted." Still, "the stones remain less real to those who cannot / name them." The role of the poet is to articulate the meaning that is "graven in silica."

That meaning is not always comforting. In "Beware of Things in Duplicate," for example, he warns us that there is "nothing so familiar / or so close that it cannot betray you." The sea, in a sensitive and unflinching poem on his uncle's time in the Merchant Marines, is an "undisguised illusion" that saves his uncle from his "icons of happiness" until, that is, he is "burned beyond recognition." "Jacob / never climbed the ladder / burning in his dream," Gioia writes in "The Burning Ladder." He "slept / through it all, a stone / upon a stone pillow, / shivering. Gravity / always greater than desire." Life is an accumulation of choices, which narrow over time. We always "must choose again," Gioia writes in "Nothing Is Lost," "but over less."

There are no easy truths here—no pat abstractions that insult or offer relief, as the case may be, while simultaneously puffing the poet's ego. Poetry is not a game—or not *merely* a game—for "kids in workshops / who care less about being poets than contributors." It's the "music" of "common speech" that might, Gioia writes in a line that rivals the best of Wallace Stevens, "direct a friend / precisely to an unknown place."

But if poetry points us to the mystery of small things and "unknown places," it also remembers who we were (or weren't) and reminds us how we became the people we didn't want to become. This storytelling function of poetry is one that is sometimes derided by contemporary sophisticates proud of their enlightened denial of both the self and sequence, but it's a tradition that goes back to the origin of the art itself. In *99 Poems*, we have short verse narratives that begin with a dead body or a visit to a family home and trace attempts to escape the past or restart lives, both of which turn out to be dreams as universal as they are illusory. "My love, how time makes hardness shine," he writes in "Sea Pebbles: An Elegy." Memory, he writes in "Summer Storm," "insists on pining / For places it never went."

In "Style," one of the new poems in the volume, Gioia writes that "Most lives consist of choosing the wrong things. / We try to compensate by choosing more, / As if sheer mass bestowed integrity." The wrong things are often the big things, and in "Most Journeys Come to This," which was originally titled "Instructions for the Afternoon," Gioia tells us to leave "the safe distractions of the masterpiece":

> Leave the museums. Find the dark churches
> in back towns that history has forgotten,
> the unimportant places the powerful ignore
> where commerce knows no profit will be made.
> Sad hamlets at the end of silted waterways,
> dry mountain villages where time
> is the thin shadow of an ancient tower
> that moves across the sundazed pavement of the square
> and disappears each evening without trace.

After all, it is in such "unimportant places" that we might find what we've "come for thoughtlessly, / shoved off into a corner." But if not—even if "the vision fails"—"this, too, could be / the revelation": that such "insufficiencies," even in art, "make up the world," and, more soberingly, that "most journeys come to this: the sun / bright on the unfamiliar hills, new vistas / dazzling the eye, the stubborn heart unchanged."

Beauty will not save the world. Poetry is only momentarily therapeutic and should offer no ticket to an easy, self-congratulatory, pseudo-spiritual "human flourishing." Rather, like both the church and nature's stones, it either speaks to us or reflects a future of "graceless frescos" among a "shadowland of marble tombs."

A lot of art, Gioia writes in "The Haunted" is "grand, authentic, second rate." *99 Poems*, as the title itself indicates, shows a poet who couldn't care less about the first two—at least not in the cavalier way that they are used today—in over thirty years of writing first-rate work.

www.ingramcontent.com/pod-product-compliance
Lightning Source LLC
Chambersburg PA
CBHW022121160426
43197CB00009B/1106